THE ERA THAT TIME FORGOT

THE ERA THAT TIME FORGOT

VOLUME ONE

B. Harrison Smith

BearManor Media
2024

THE ERA THAT TIME FORGOT
VOLUME ONE

© *2024 B. Harrison Smith*

All rights reserved.

Published in the United States of America by:

BearManor Media

1317 Edgewater Dr. #110
Orlando, FL 32804

bearmanormedia.com

Printed in the United States.

Typesetting and layout by PKJ Passion Global

ISBN—979-8-88771-375-5

DEDICATION

For everyone who loves to have fun watching movies.
There was a time when that happened.

TABLE OF CONTENTS

"All of those [old movies and TV shows] thrilled me in the same way that seeing the hyper-realistic dinosaurs of the *Jurassic Park* franchise thrilled me, so to me it was less about the CGI and more about imagining a world in which you could interact with the dinosaurs."

-- **Author Chris Cevasco**
Episode 155
Geek's Guide to the Galaxy **podcast.**

FOREWORD

Tane McClure

As the daughter of actor Doug McClure, the world of make-believe, including huge dinosaurs and ancient worlds seems perfectly normal to me. Growing up, I was always eager to see and hear about all of my father's fantastical and exciting adventures as an actor.

In my teens, I traveled to London, England, to spend time with my father while he was filming *The People That Time Forgot*, about an incredible hidden world filled with scary man-eating dinosaurs and ancient civilizations. My father had previously starred in *At the Earth's Core*, and *The Land That Time Forgot* several years before. I must say that I thought all the dinosaurs in these films were exceptionally cool for their time.

Courtesy Tane McClure Arendts

These movies were produced at Pinewood studios where my father built a strong friendship with Producer John Dark and Director Kevin Connor. There was a family-like atmosphere at Pinewood and director Kevin Connor continued that feeling brilliantly on his film set. This suited my father perfectly, as he was never one to play into the self-absorbed nature of some stars. He was humble and appreciative of the honor that was given to him as a successful actor.

He worked hard and enjoyed his craft in the process. Movies are meant to be fun, and one should have fun making them. This is exactly the impression I got from my father about his experiences with director Kevin Connor.

Kevin also directed my father in several more films including *Warlords of Atlantis*, and *The House Where Evil Dwells*.

Courtesy Tane McClure Arendts

I recently watched *At the Earth's Core* again and I was struck by how the film pulls you in. I felt like I was literally traveling with him into the *Earth's Core*. A spectacular imaginary world that we could only barely fathom if it had not been for Kevin Connor's extraordinary works.

My father passed away from cancer in 1995, and I miss him terribly, but when I see him in these films, to me… he is alive again. He is traveling in time to unknown lands forever. This is what a great film should do, take the viewer to a place where we can dream and be inspired. For me, it is a place where my father lives on.

To my father's dear friend Kevin Connor… my father felt that you were such a talented and likeable director to work with. He enjoyed every moment. And I thank you, for this gift of seeing my father live on in your films and for your spectacular cinematic achievements that inspires us all. As a new feature film director, myself, I hope to walk in your footsteps.

Thank you to B. Harrison Smith for writing *The Era That Time Forgot* that reminds us of the history of filmmaking, and the true meaning behind it...to inspire...to thrill...with JOY... and FRIENDSHIP.

Oh yes... Let's not forget the cool monsters and dinosaurs. Gotta have them!

Tane McClure October, 2023

Courtesy Tane McClure Arendts

INTRODUCTION

"I don't have a lot of memories of my father when I was a boy. My parents split around 1973, and he came to take my younger brother and me every Sunday for a while. It was the *Gen X Divorce Package*: Pick up around ten in the morning with drop off sometime around seven at night. That often wound up being our grandmother's house, where our mother would fetch us.

It was a long day, and I already hated Sundays because they came after Saturday--which was the thrill of no school, Saturday morning cartoons and shows, and long days playing with friends. That consisted of journeys far from home to the slate quarries that bordered our small post-WWII town of East Bangor or its sprawling dam filled with giant snails and millions of turtles.

Sometimes we hung out on the tracks to throw rocks at the train cars as they passed. It was a world also filled with dinosaur battles and Godzilla-era kaiju as we pretended the slate mountains we scaled concealed massive monsters beneath them.

I put together a group to travel to the center of the earth after finding large passageways in the slate hills, convinced it would lead me to a land that time forgot at the earth's core.

We watched *Land of the Lost* on *NBC* and monster movies on creature double feature Saturdays. No wonder Sundays sucked... how do you top that when you're seven?

The old man had his "divorce apartment" with no woods or slate quarry monster cairns. Instead, it was three channels of "Nothing on Sundays TV," no games, and nothing to do.

The only film I remember seeing with my pre-divorce father was a drive-in double feature of *The Sting* and *The Doberman Gang*, and I barely can recall all of that.

After the divorce, he took us to the matinee movies quite a bit. It was an easy way to kill a couple of hours with the kids. The benefit to this was he didn't want to sit through "kiddie shows." No *Disney* or cartoons or animated films (which was fine by both of us). The old man wanted to see stuff that wouldn't cause too much mental suffering.

That's how I saw *The Land That Time Forgot* in its US theatrical release in 1975. We went to the Eric Twin in Easton, PA, and I loved it. I wanted to see it again right after the first show, but my dad said no.

Until that time, dinosaurs were either stop-motion or men in suits. *Land's* dinosaurs were different. While today I know they were puppets, they were revolutionary to me in that theater in 1975. We had dinosaurs eating people, guns blazing, and dinosaurs even fighting each other.

I never saw anything quite like it, and I kept fond memories of the film as I grew up. We didn't have cable, and we did not have a VCR until Reagan's second term, so it wasn't like I could catch the film again easily. You had to watch for it when it came to regular TV, and then it was hit or miss.

This was a time when there were three networks, the broadcasting day ended around midnight or not long after, and you had a TV guide to tell you what would be playing. You had no control over the content you wanted to see.

The old man took us to see *King Kong* in 1976. The ballyhooed remake of the 1933 classic was brought to us by Dino DeLaurentiis, the Italian producer who threw lots of money and hype at almost everything he did. He wanted to top *Jaws*, and his "monkey" (as he called it) or "his Kong" would beat that shark.

"Nobody cries when Jaws die," he told a reporter in his broken English. "When my Kong dies, people cry."

He wasn't wrong on that one. The problem with *King Kong* 1976 was that it wasn't all that much fun. The 1933 film was chock full of dinosaurs and giant beasts and packed in far more thrills and suspense.

We got some impressive "guy in an ape suit" effects and miniature work, but the only other beast on Kong's island seemed to be this giant, fake rubber snake that brought laughs in the theater. Kong's fight with the T-Rex in the 1933 film had become iconic. He broke that lizard's massive jaws like they were balsa wood. He did it again in the Rankin-Bass 1967 *King Kong Escapes* with Gorosaurus.

I thought for sure we were going to get some sweet ape-lizard combat in this big, expensive theatrical remake. The press promised a full-sized ape robot to portray Kong. That was not true, and I guess I need to correct myself here. They didn't exactly promise Kong would be a robot throughout the whole movie, but they didn't deny it either. There were lots of articles on how this giant, 50-foot mechanical ape was made to play Kong.

THE ERA THAT TIME FORGOT • 17

They really did do that, but if you watch the film, it appears for a whole ten seconds in the film and looks nothing like Rick Baker's award-winning ape suit that portrayed Kong. Like I said, everything was BIG with Dino, and *King Kong* was no exception.

This was the early '70s--the era of the disaster epic, and *Kong* had to deliver. The problem was…it didn't. I left the theater disappointed. Yeah, I cried like Dino promised when the ape got blasted off the World Trade Center (but not killed as we would find out in the abysmal *King Kong Lives* ten years later) but otherwise, I left unmoved. The movie might've been big and expensive, but it just wasn't that much fun.

It wasn't like *The Land That Time Forgot*, which had me wanting to walk right back into the theater and watch it all over again. A movie made for a fraction of *Kong's* budget entertained me far more and delighted for years to come unlike Dino's monkey.

When I heard they made a sequel to *The Land That Time Forgot* a few years later, and my aunt and uncle said they were taking me to see it, I couldn't wait for the day to end so we could get to the drive-in to see it along with At *the Earth's Core*. Both films did not disappoint.

Three years later, I would see another film by the director of these dinosaur masterpieces and felt like the rug was pulled out from under me. I saw *Motel Hell* in the same drive-in as *People That Time Forgot* and *At the Earth's Core*; only that film was nothing like director Kevin Connor's dinosaur movies.

Motel Hell scared the shit out of me, and I had nightmares about it for weeks. The image of those people buried up to their heads and force-fed in the garden haunted me ever since, and director Kevin Connor's name was as seared into my brain just as indelibly as Steven Spielberg's would become.

I've been told I have an incredible memory. Details that escape most people seem a matter of course for me. I can remember the weather of certain days decades ago and where I was when this event or that event happened.

I remember it was cold and rainy when I saw *The Land That Time Forgot*, and I even remember it was cold and snowy when I saw *King Kong* two years later. However, it was a perfect end of the summer night in 1977 when I thrilled to that double header of *People That Time Forgot* and *At the Earth's Core*. I held hands with a pretty girl atop my aunt and uncle's 1974 *T-Bird*, and I can remember how orange and red the sky was, waiting for it to grow dark enough for the screen in that packed drive-in to light up.

That's filmmaking, folks.

None of the films I mentioned (even *King Kong*) had effects that would come close to the digital wonders of the *Jurassic Park* films. That's not the point. They gave me memories…wonderful memories because they were experiences.

It was all about the effects or painstaking analysis of budgets and how the movie magic was done "behind the scenes" that has now helped to ruin the movie-going experience.

Online movie conversations are often verbal assaults and venom-spewing arguments instead of fun, fond remembrances, and appreciation for the medium and what it does bind us culturally. The Internet has helped to splinter us, divide us and make us angry as hell toward each other over movies.

There was a time when you were excited by the TV spots and commercials. There were no detailed "making of" specials or DVD extras to give away all of the secrets. You got this cool commercial between your TV shows, and that ignited the "Mom! Can we go see…" factor.

You knew if you didn't catch it in the theater, you were going to miss out. There was no "I'll stream it, rent it, pay per view it" later. You saw it in the theaters or you didn't see it at all.

It was time just before the casual consumption of film and easy access. You had to savor what you got in the theaters and be content until it was thrown on TV years later.

The age of immediate gratification with movies has taken that away from us. It's not about savoring cuisine or even sinking our teeth into a nice piece of junk food. Remember when *McDonald's* and such were TREATS not staples of the dinner table? Remember how good that shit tasted on the few occasions you got hold of it?

Now it's part of many regular diets, and the thrill is gone.

The Land That Time Forgot and other films like it were not cuisine. They didn't aim for that. They were juicy hamburgers and shakes with some fries, and you loved them. You ate them up and wanted more. That's what the filmmakers set out to do. They didn't take their hamburgers and pass them off as steak like many films do today.

I will argue many big budget effects films are really nothing more than bad films with big budgets. There is very little that separates *The Meg* movies from the *Sharknado* movies except the money spent on them.

The thing is I don't find those giant-budgeted films fun. I can say without hesitation I would (and have) sit through multiple viewings of *The Land That Time Forgot* over any of the *Jurassic Park/World* films because those mega-budgeted franchise films become tedious after a while. They lose what little fun they had, and I will stand by my belief that the original *Jurassic Park* is still the best of them all because its heart and soul were aligned with films like *The Land That Time Forgot*.

I wrote a book on the making of 1977's *The Last Dinosaur* which likely got made because of the success of Connor's *The Land That Time Forgot*. People demanded dinosaurs, and they were everywhere in the '70s. I looked at WHY *The Last Dinosaur* still resonates with people who were kids when they saw it on *The ABC Friday Night Movie*.

I am going to do the same thing here. Kevin Connor gave us some very special films, and while two of them showed up on *Mystery Science Theater 3000*, that should be looked at as a badge of honor.

The two *MST3K* episodes featuring The *Land That Time Forgot* and *At the Earth's Core* just might be the best of the entire series (which ran over two decades). I stand by the fact that *The Land That Time Forgot* is my favorite because...they got it.

The show writers got the fun these movies gave and the crazy inventiveness that went behind them to get them to the screen. The riffing commentary by Jonah Ray, Tom Servo, and Crow is hilarious because it is supported by the absolute fun of those films. It's easy to riff on them because they were made so well and, most of all...so damned entertaining.

To provide contrast, the last season of the show, headlined by Patton Oswalt called *The Gauntlet*, also features a "mockbuster" film from the infamous low budget studio *The Asylum* called *Atlantic Rim*. It's a CGI rip-off movie of the big budget *Pacific Rim* and made to cash in on that film's name brand. *The Asylum* movies can be often equated to remoras affixing themselves to the jaw of a shark; they are there for the ride and to feed off the scraps from their host.

That episode is not really that funny because that film (which really is a spoof for all intents and purposes) isn't fun. It wasn't entertaining before *MST3K* got a hold of it.

That's why I turned that episode off halfway through. There just wasn't anything fun about it in its original form, so the riffing soundtrack with Jonah and the boys fell flat.

It's the material, folks.

Kevin Connor's films are not cynical. They are fun because they were made by people who loved movies, who still were kids at heart, and most of all…gave a shit about what they were doing. Many had hard world experience in World War II…they saw things and that translated into their craft.

This is what moved me to write this series of books on a director that entertained me, scared me, and today makes me wish I had the honor to work for. At the very least, I get to learn from him in interviewing him and writing his story.

We owe a debt of thanks to Kevin Connor and his teams, and they are the people time should not forget.

DON'T LOSE YOUR DINOSAUR

"When I was a kid, when I was a little boy, I always wanted to be a dinosaur. I wanted to be a Tyrannosaurus Rex more than anything in the world. I made my arms short and I roamed the backyard, I chased the neighborhood cats, I growled and I roared. Everybody knew me and was afraid of me. And one day my dad said, "Bobby, you are 17. It's time to throw childish things aside," and I said, "Okay, Pop." But he didn't really say that, he said, "Stop being a fucking dinosaur and get a job…The point is, don't lose your dinosaur."
-- **Dr. Robert Doback,** *Stepbrothers,* **2008**

I wanted to be Godzilla. I wanted the power of atomic breath and to wade through skyscrapers while my enemies tried in vain to stop me. I wanted to find my own secret world populated with fantastical creatures and to be lost in it. My early childhood was marred by the ugly divorce of my parents and after that a brief period of physical and verbal abuse from my mother's boyfriend. I was bullied in elementary school. My house was built in 1900, had a dirt floor basement with rats tunneling in from the nearby dump recently shut down and purged.

I wanted to be Ichiro from *Godzilla's Revenge* and fly away to Monster Island where I could live among the beasts and escape the real world. I wanted to know there was something better out there.

Movies allowed me that escape, but there was something else going on in America at that time.

The early 1970s saw a "back to basics" movement emerging in America, characterized by a desire to embrace a simpler, self-sufficient lifestyle and reconnect with nature. This movement was often associated with the idea of "living off the land," where individuals sought to be more self-reliant and reduce their reliance on modern conveniences and consumer culture. Several factors contributed to the surge of interest in this lifestyle, and it was influenced by generational shifts, particularly among the Baby Boomer generation.

The 1970s was a decade marked by various countercultural movements that challenged mainstream values. The anti-establishment sentiment of the 1960s spilled over into the next decade, leading many individuals to reject the materialistic and consumer-driven society. The back-to-basics movement was, in part, a reaction to the perceived excesses and conformity of modern urban life.

The decade saw a growing awareness of environmental issues, such as pollution, deforestation, and the depletion of natural resources. Many individuals felt a deep concern for the planet's well-being and sought to adopt lifestyles that minimized their ecological footprint. Living off the land, in harmony with nature, became a way to align personal choices with environmental values.

This will be reflected in the dinosaur movies that I remember. The plots were almost always focused around the clash of worlds: industrial, cold modern meets Eden-like throwback nature. The rapid industrialization and urbanization of America led to the loss of rural traditions and agricultural practices. The back-to-basics movement represented a longing to reclaim those roots and reconnect with a simpler way of life, reminiscent of earlier generations and rural communities.

The Land That Time Forgot's lost continent of Caprona was this unspoiled place save for the proto-human element which was also depicted as despoiling the land. When modern man (1914 modern man at least) arrived, they immediately started shooting, killing and blowing shit up.

The crew find crude oil and in no time set up a makeshift refinery that belches black plumes into the air. The film's conclusion gave us an erupting volcano that seemed to almost purge the land of these modern parasites that brought death and destruction to this once pristine continent. The same themes will hold true in *The People That Time Forgot*.

Just before the 70s, *King Kong Escapes* hinted toward modern man's despoiling of nature. When non-islanders infiltrate Kong's island, they start killing the peaceful natives, drop bombs on the land and kidnap Kong, the island's god. Modern man wrecks everything and is an enemy to the earth and its natural balance.

Richard Boone and Joan Van Ark's *The Last Dinosaur* followed this template. Another dinosaur lost world isolated by ice (this time under the northern polar ice caps) also saw modern man wrecking things the moment they entered the lost realm. Boone wanted to start killing even though he said he won't and looked for any excuse to do so.

Whereas a sub brought *Land's* people to the lost world, a laser drill powered Polar Borer brings Boone and company to Dino Land with similar results. All *The Last Dinosaur* needed was a volcanic eruption at the end.

Even TV's *Land of the Lost* had similar themes. Marshall, Will and Holly brought disruption to the balance of things by falling into the parallel prehistoric world. A number of episodes focused on the restoration of balance with the merging of past and present universes.

The family was forced to live off the land in a cave, a back to basics thing that both *The Land That Time Forgot* and *The Last Dinosaur* utilized.

The 70s witnessed economic and energy crises, including the OPEC oil embargo of 1973-1974. These events led to soaring energy prices and economic hardships for many Americans. Embracing a self-sufficient lifestyle allowed individuals to become less dependent on external factors and cope with the uncertainty of the times.

There was a surge in "return to the old days" kind of films outside of dinosaurs. Robert Redford's *Jeremiah Johnson, Across the Great Divide, The Adventures of the Wilderness Family* and *Grizzly Adams* to name a few; all reflected modern man against more primitive and simpler elements.

Communal living and alternative communities became popular. Many young people sought to create intentional communities where they could live collectively, share resources, and grow their own food. These communities fostered a spirit of cooperation, self-sufficiency, and a desire to escape the trappings of mainstream society.

As for the generational aspect, the Boomers played a significant role in driving the back-to-basics movement. Born between the mid-1940s and the mid-60s, many Boomers were coming of age in the 1970s. This generation was known for its desire for social change, idealism, and a rejection of traditional norms. Boomers were drawn to the idea of living closer to nature, embracing a DIY ethos, and seeking a more authentic and meaningful existence.

While the back-to-basics movement saw significant popularity in the 1970s, it gradually waned in subsequent decades. As the economic situation improved, and energy prices stabilized, the urgency for self-sufficiency and frugality diminished.

The 1980s marked a period of economic prosperity and consumerism, which shifted societal values back toward materialism and individual success. The rise of technology and modern conveniences made urban living more appealing to many, reducing the need or desire for self-sufficiency. As Baby Boomers aged, priorities and responsibilities shifted, leading to a focus on careers, family, and traditional lifestyles.

This rise of technology and movement toward the digital era as well as the birth of the modern blockbuster with *Jaws* in 1975; brought us to *Jurassic Park* and a resurgence in dinosaur interest but instead of it being humans find lost worlds, they created them through the wonders of computers and genetics.

The digital era gave us digital dinosaurs and it all stemmed from the previous decades and the "old school" ways of the 1970s and before.

A fresh wave of cinematic mavericks emerged in 70s cinema, giving rise to what would be known as New Hollywood. Gone were the classic studio formulas; in came edgier stories, grittier realism, and complex characters. The curtains opened to classics like *The Godfather* (1972), *A Clockwork Orange* (1971), Stanley Kubrick's audacious dive into dystopia, shocking viewers with its violence and social commentary. The film raised eyebrows, but it also pushed the boundaries of cinematic expression, becoming a cult classic in its own right.

The 70s introduced a new fascination with antiheroes and unconventional protagonists. Moviegoers cheered for the bad guys, embracing their rebellious spirit and love for the outlaw. In *Dirty Harry* (1971), Clint Eastwood's no-nonsense detective took justice into his own hands, becoming an iconic symbol of tough justice in the urban jungle.

We saw this in *The Land That Time Forgot* where Doug McClure's Tyler Bowen is really an anti-hero. He hijacks the German sub, supersedes its captain and starts killing dinosaurs almost as soon as he gets inside Caprona. McClure takes matters into his own hands and becomes a rebel. This will serve him well in the final moments of the film.

In the midst of the 70s cinematic revolution, moviegoers found themselves immersed in a whirlwind of genres, stories, and emotions. From the crime-ridden streets of New York, prehistoric continents and islands to the far reaches of space, the 70s were a cinematic rollercoaster ride unlike any other and dinosaurs ruled.

Ever since the advent of movie theaters, prehistoric creatures have roared their way into our hearts, captivating audiences young and old alike. But what is it about dinosaur films that has kept us enthralled for generations?

In the early days of cinema, pioneering filmmakers recognized the allure of these ancient giants, unleashing them on the silver screen in all their colossal glory. From the stop-motion magic of Willis O'Brien's *The Lost World* (1925) to Ray Harryhausen's masterpieces like *One Million Years B.C.* (1966), dinosaurs became icons of the cinematic landscape.

The original *Lost World* (not to be confused with the *Jurassic Park* sequel) set the stage for *King Kong* less than a decade later. *The Lost World's* landscape was an isolated, elevated plateau in South America. No ice walls or polar caps. Modern man comes, conquers and takes.

The film sees the capture of a Brontosaurus and transported back to London where it wreaks havoc upon escaping. We will see New York go through this with Kong's rampage. The story template was set and it would barrel toward the 70s and peak dinosaur movie.

Dinosaur films transported us to a realm untouched by modern concerns. Who wouldn't want to trade deadlines for a thrilling

chase with a T-Rex or leave traffic jams for the freedom of a ptero-
dactyl's flight? These films offer a dose of escapism with a side of
primeval adventure.

As a boy I can attest to this escapism. Running from a T-Rex was
preferable to running from my mother's boyfriend who promised to
kick my ass after knocking a tooth out of my head.

I think there is also something tragic and doomed about dinosaur movies. The endings are almost always the same—the world
is engulfed in some kind of cataclysm. It's a reminder that the great
beasts had their time and then it was over.

Kind of like us.

Jurassic Park will make it clear that "dinosaurs had their shot"
and more and more it looks like the same can be said about humans.
The "back to the land" desire of the 70s might have been some kind
of subconscious collective reckoning that we've ruined everything
and slit our own throats.

It won't be a volcano or an asteroid that wipes us out, it will
be by our own hand. We are a doomed species just like the dinosaurs before us that ruled this planet for almost a hundred million years.

The Land That Time Forgot and Connor's other films tap into
all of this. Time is always moving forward even when it looks backward and everything has its time. All things end.

Dinosaur films give us a rare glimpse into a distant past where
nature's grandest creations ruled the Earth. They transport us to
epochs beyond our own, forging a connection with history on an
epic scale. Themes of survival, adaptation, and the consequences of
human interference resonate with our modern sensibilities. These
colossal beings teach us about the delicate balance of ecosystems,

reminding us to cherish our own world and the creatures that inhabit it.

Ask your grandparents, parents, and siblings, and they'll likely have a favorite dinosaur movie etched in their memory. These films span generations, creating shared experiences and fond memories. A dinosaur film is more than just a flick; it becomes a part of our cultural fabric, passed down like a treasured heirloom.

I saw Connor's films with just as many adults in the audience as there were kids. These films tapped into their inner child as well. The *Jurassic Park/World franchise* was not built off of just kiddie matinee audiences. The adults drove the ticket sales because they never lost their dinosaur.

Neither did Kevin Connor.

GETTING INTO THE BUSINESS

Kevin Connor was born in Kings Cross, London, on July 14, 1937, on the eve of World War II. "I was brought home to North Mimms, in Hertfordshire. North Mimms is a very small hamlet but I was brought up in Hertfordshire countryside – as it happened - not far from Elstree Studios."

In our first conversation, he marveled at the impact of technology on the filmmaking industry. Having grown up before the atomic age, living through the space age and seeing the dawn of the digital age, Connor finds today's filmmaking power incredible.

"You don't need to come up the ranks for twenty years anymore," he told me. "Now it's all downloadable; you can shoot on an iPhone and edit on a computer. No more cutting room blocks and camaraderie, the indecipherable sounds of clattering moviolas and synchronizers sounds that emit through the corridors as you dash back and forth to the joining rooms. No smell of film or film cement anymore. Now you can do it all from home. If you're computer savvy, you're off to the races."

He acknowledged that who sees your films is important. "I don't know if YouTube gets you up the ladder, but you definitely have more avenues today to show your work. It's sure a different time."

"You had to find those great foreign films in London because there weren't that many cinemas in London in the 50s that catered to that market. You couldn't just get a copy of any film you wanted like today. There were few books on filmmaking, and I was interested in film cameras and editing."

There was one book on editing at that time, Connor said. His interest in editing and film started in the closing of the 1940s and early 1950s, and that book was Karel Reisz's "The Technique of Film Editing" co-authored with Gavin Millar.

Karel Reisz, a trailblazing figure in the world of cinema, emerged as a renowned filmmaker and an advocate for the art of film editing. Connor would go on to work with this legend.

Reisz's life journey took him from war-torn Europe to the bustling streets of London, where he left an indelible mark on the film industry.

This will become a major theme of Connor's career as the people he worked with had their careers shaped by their experiences during the war.

"The Technique of Film Editing" demystified the art of editing; delving into the nuances of visual storytelling, rhythm, and the creative decisions that shape a film's narrative. Reisz's contributions to the book drew from his experiences as a director and his collaborations with editors, providing a holistic understanding of the collaborative process between the director and editor.

"That was The Bible in those days," Connor confirmed. "Other than that, there were books by film stars and a little bit about the industry, but this [Reisz's book] was really the only reference material of merit. It was all you could find back then."

Connor reflected on his school days and thinking that he never thought there were actual jobs in the film industry—jobs where one could make a full-time living. He remembers materials posted in one of his primary school classes. "There was this photo of someone on a film crane. A cameraman, something like that, looking down on the crowd, whatever, and I thought, I would like to do that." He lamented again that there just wasn't a lot of places to get information.

He got his first still film camera around the age of twelve.

I understood what he was saying as my high school years drew to a close by the mid-80s and I tried to select a school for filmmaking. There just weren't that many and most of all there were few resources for helping me to decide.

When I went into the guidance department to talk to my counselor at the end of my sophomore year, I spent almost fifteen minutes explaining to him that I wanted to do FILMMAKING not photography, and when this was finally conveyed all he did was refer me to a stack of catalogues over on a table.

Sounds like things didn't change in the 40 years Kevin Connor looked for a future in this industry. As with his situation, the 80s did not offer up a bevy of resource materials. There was no Internet to hop on and explore a college's site. There was nothing to let you explore their full film programs, or most of all reach out to graduates who went on into the industry.

You had a stack of catalogues and almost all roads led to NYU, UCLA, or USC. That was pretty much it. I ended up selecting Penn State University without even knowing exactly what their "film major" entailed. For all I knew, I would graduate with a degree in film theory or criticism and do nothing with actual hands-on film-making.

It wasn't like Penn State was known for its film program or is today.

Connor's parents were supportive of their son. "They were very kind and generous people." His father started work as a Chartered Surveyor/Architect and rose to be Deputy Surveyor for The Metro-politan Water Board of London.

"I suppose you would call my mother a 'home maker,' but she built some dog – kennels and boarded animals to earn a small amount of extra income. Both of them came from a working-class district of Colliers Wood/Wimbledon in SW19 area of London."

Courtesy Kevin Connor

Courtesy MGM

Young Kevin Connor with
A borrowed Bell & Howell
camera, embarking down the
road toward making movies.

Courtesy Kevin Connor

While I was born in Kings Cross, my parents lived about 25 miles north of London. I was brought up in the countryside. It was not far from Borehamwood, Elstree Studios, and in those days MGM had a studio there. I used to drive past as I grew up. They were shooting all of those Elizabeth Taylor and knight movies there and you could see it happening from the hillsides. It was fascinating."

Connor grew up in rural Hertfotdshire and made money mowing lawns and working a newspaper round. He was kind of a "farm kid" having worked with agriculture machinery such as threshers and the like. "We had a small holding in the back garden which held pigs and chickens and geese and things. During the war years, we always had fresh food—eggs, meats, and nutritional stuff; we were very lucky."

There was rationing during this time while London endured "The Blitz" from Hitler's air force. "We had this stuff the government doled out called Cod Liver Oil and it was awful, although nutritious. A mixture called 'Concentrated Orange Juice' was a wonderful relief. In those days it was pretty basic and the MOF (Ministry of Food), also supplied gruel - a kind of porridge - but it wasn't. As children, we never had sugar, sweets, or bananas until after the war ended."

Connor went to the local school in the nearby town of Potter's Bar until 1948 when he moved to a Comprehensive middle school.

He recalled that there was a vocational aspect to his education. "You were exposed to both sides--academic and trade work. By the time you got to fifth grade they would stream us into the proper avenues they felt we should go. I became more interested in the art side of life."

His parents were supportive but also hands-off. "My father was a rather distant kind of guy. Very kind, very gentle, but at times remote. My mother was also a good parent and found extra education for me from a retired head schoolmistress who lived opposite.

My father introduced me to a film director who was living in a nearby town. This was a guy called Darrel Catling.

"We went over there one Sunday for tea and sat down. Darrel talked about his career in documentaries. He had made films at the famous Pinewood Studios."

Connor explained that the studios and this filmmaker used a new technique for filming called an "Independent Frame."

The "Independent Frame" technique in filmmaking refers to a specific approach used in constructing and filming movie sets, particularly on sound stages. This technique involves creating self-contained, freestanding set pieces that can be easily moved, rearranged, or reconfigured as needed to accommodate various camera angles and shot compositions. Each set piece is essentially an independent frame within the larger stage, allowing filmmakers to capture shots from different perspectives without needing to reconstruct the entire set.

This technique streamlines the filmmaking process by minimizing the need for extensive set changes between shots. It allows for quicker adjustments and reduces downtime, enabling the crew to focus on capturing the desired shots.

Directors and cinematographers can easily capture shots from various angles within the same set without compromising continuity. This technique is particularly useful for scenes that require multiple perspectives, such as dialogue exchanges or action sequences.

While the initial construction of the independent frames may require additional planning and resources, the overall cost can be reduced compared to building multiple separate sets for each shot.

This would be important when Connor helmed The Land That Time Forgot and other films working with his director of photography.

"They would wheel this whole set onto a stage." Catling directed two of those

films, but his career focused more on documentary-type films."

This networking bore fruit when Catling invited Connor to lunch in Soho and meet a director who was leaving the world of documentaries to direct his first feature film 'Cosh Boy." The director was Lewis Gilbert who later became a director of several Bond films and many other memorable features.

"A hero and later a friend."

Not being in the film industry in shape or form --Darrel Catling was really the only contact his father managed to introduce Connor to.

Connor had his lunch with Gilbert. He listened to the director's experiences and aspirations and was really the only contact his father introduced to him.

However he did find later that his father would regularly visit Shepperton Studios as part of his job's purview. Connor later in life found that his father bought a portable dressing room from the studio that allegedly belonged to a famous actress at the time, Anna Neagle.

"He bought this thing and had it delivered back to home where it became my little shed when I was 13 or 14."

The dressing room was installed in the back garden and named 'Anna Neagle.'

His father didn't push him to go into the film industry, but he didn't dissuade him either. Connor knew by 1950-51 he wanted to be in film. "I was filming the school sports and stuff like that. I didn't enjoy sports, never being good at them."

The teen had a paper route. He talked to a shop owner on this route who happened to have a film camera. He told Kevin he could borrow it any time.

"He showed me this 9.5mm camera. While bigger than 8mm it was a lot less than 16mm. I used it to film the school sports. He was very helpful."

Connor's mother wasn't able to comprehend what kind of job her son could get in the film industry. "She was lovely and helped in my education."

Connor admitted he wasn't very good at math or science as a student. "I wasn't a particularly bright student. I was sort of lumpy and overweight." With that said Connor laid out that he frequented the nearby Ritz Cinema for Saturday morning movies. It was his first real exposure to movies as a boy and he recalled Erroll Flynn's Robin Hood being his first movie.

"It was only a shilling to get in," he chuckled.

It was that borrowed camera that got him interested in shooting film and working in the medium through filming school sports. He did manage to rope other kids into being in his films.

"During the war, the Americans built a hospital in the country-side near where we lived because of the up-coming D-Day landings.

We used to bicycle down to this hospital and we would meet the soldiers where we would get sweets and bananas and things like that, some things we had never seen. Anyway, a year or two after the war ended there was this great big light coming from where this hospital used to be.

We cycled down to it and discovered that some people were making a movie. A film company had turned the derelict American hospital - into Belsen – the horrendous Nazi Concentration Camp. It was night time and there were these poor people tramping through the infamous gates. Nazi soldiers yelling – Alsatian dogs on leashes barking – a chimney emitting smoke. It was a memorable image, yet under the glare of the lights –an absolutely mind-bending transition from what the site used to be.

A film set at night is magic. It stops your heart sometimes."

That was a major push for Connor to think of the film industry as a career. One of the people coming through this fake concentration camp was none other than actress Anna Neagle, whose old dressing room had become Connor's activity shed. Her husband, Herbert Wilcox was the director.

It was a small world set.

With Americans stationed throughout post-war England. Kevin's parents made friends with a number of them. This opened a pipeline to American magazines and publications. He found a comic in one of the publications called "The Sad Sack" and thought it might make good material for one of his first films.

"The Sad Sack" was a classic American comic strip created by Sgt. George Baker during World War II. The strip revolved around the misadventures of an inept and bumbling soldier named Sad Sack. With his perpetually downcast expression and knack for finding himself in comically disastrous situations, Sad Sack became an endearing and relatable character to readers.

"I collared a few of my school chums to be in this but it didn't pan out very well." He laughed at the silliness of it and then remembered that his school would organize movie outings.

Despite all this Connor and friend took the opportunity to sneak into the theaters despite their cheap admission prices.

"We'd sometimes go through the toilets to get in."

Graduation soon came on the horizon.

"Come 1953, my last year in school, I wrote to every film company in the London telephone directory. Anything that had film or photography in its title, I wrote. I wrote about a hundred of these letters and got about 15-20 back saying there were no openings. All negative replies.

I went back to school to further myself in an art program and two weeks later my headmaster gets a phone call from my mother. She relayed information to be given to me I went to the headmaster's office where he told me there was a film company in London 's Soho, who wanted to see me, possibly employ me.

Connor went off the next day for an interview to be a trainee in the cutting or editing rooms. It was a foot in the door as he saw it. "Once you're in, you're in," Connor thought. It was a documentary company, not feature films, but to Kevin Connor, it was a first step.

Writing to everybody got him his first job.

"You learn more in one week on a film set than you would in four years of a film school."

THE ROAD TO CAPRONA

Kevin Connor left school at sixteen to go work for *British Films*—a unique production company that made commercials but also showed films via a fleet of single-decker buses.

"They would show films in poorer areas and they would project the film on the back of the bus. They would drive to the location, set the bus up, people would bring their chairs and sit in the street and watch the film. They would project the movie, like back projection, onto something they made on the back of the bus—a screen. People would sit outside on the street in the evenings and watch these films."

Connor went on to say the company would do this for schools as well. "They would come to one, setting up the same way to show documentaries and the odd features but it was mainly instructional films and stuff like that."

This was a post-war attempt by the British government to bring some kind of normalcy back into the lives of a society devastated by Hitler's Blitz and another generation lost to world war.

He would sit in a cutting room in London up in Soho and said he literally did nothing for six months as an office boy. While the company was making films, they weren't editing them there. Connor was in the cutting room but nothing was going on.

"There was nothing for me to do. I was making the tea, running to the head office back and forth and meeting people and such—really nothing. I would sit in this sparsely furnished cutting room, listening to "Tosher the Tie King," outside the window in Berwick Street market, selling his wares, whilst admiring an antiquated black piece of equipment known as an ACMIOLA. I had no clue how it was to be used. Quite a beast, with a single glass eye, it clearly had something to do with running 35mm film and a sound track through it. Big time and not 9.5mm!!

At this time no editor had been assigned for me to learn from and assist."

However, Connor was in London and after work he could find two or three cinemas where he could see Italian, French and American films. "The films one should see," he said.

The company actually made a couple of films. "I got to touch film, join film and smell film and smell the cement and all the rest of it." Over the next 18 months Connor got his hands dirty and learned the trade when this work came into the studio.

"Eventually wheels turned and the company made a high profile documentary film, and a wonderful man, George Fisher, was assigned as editor and he taught me so much. I got to touch film, splice film, smell film and the cement that stuck it all together. Over the next 18 months Connor got his hands dirty handling reels of film and humping them up and down Wardour Street – (being the center of the film distribution it was nick-named 'the only street shady on both sides'!)"

While not feature films, these projects allowed Connor to not just get hands-on experience; these projects opened the networking doors. All the weird sounds of a cutting room at full blast indelibly entered his brain and whilst not feature films, they allowed Connor to get hands-on experience, and slowly the projects opened networking doors.

British Films Ltd. actually produced a full length feature – for children – entitled *The Flying Eye*. It starred Julia Lockwood, the daughter of the British film star – Margaret Lockwood. The writer of the screenplay was, co-incidentally, Darrell Catling.

The editor, George Fisher, he was working for said "I know the chap in charge of the cutting rooms at Shepperton Studios. I'll call him and tell him that there's a young lad here and if anyone wants an assistant…"

The call came through about a month later from Jack Drake at Shepperton, inviting Connor to come and work on a small B-feature film. He didn't have to think twice. It was the summer of 1954.

"I gave my notice and off I went."

The film was called '*They Can't Kill Me*,' directed by the legendary Val Guest. Connor was assigned to be the assistant to the Sound Editor. Mixing and dubbing would take place at the studio as the film had been fine-cut and locked. He didn't meet any of the film production crew, but a number of major feature films were coming through Shepperton at the time, '(*Footsteps in the Fog, Cockleshell Heroes*)' as the industry picked up at long last.

"Once you meet the editors and assistants working on the other films, you're in the mix. It was really quite a small community."

From there Connor moved to Pinewood Studios after a call and invite to work there. It was a different work atmosphere at Pinewood.

"Shepperton Studios was freelance, a different mentality. You learned your trade and started to feel your way about—making sound charts and that kind of stuff. An apprenticeship if you will. Then off to Pinewood it was more of a company and rank and file organization. It was like a Freemason background. J. Arthur Rank [the studio founder] was a miller from the middle of England. It was like going to a public school. It was kind of like the poor kid coming to the school and getting roughed around a little by the rich kids."

DIRECTORS:
THE MARQUES OF LINLITHGOW, M.C.
THE RT. HON. (CHAIRMAN)
LORD CHINHAM, M.C.
H. RUSSELL SMITH
K. L. LOCKSTONE
P. B. FRERE, M.C

HEAD OFFICE
199, PICCADILLY
LONDON, W. I
TEL REGENT 2626/9

WORKS:
260, HIGH ROAD
BALHAM, S.W.17
TEL. BALHAM 6677/8

YOUR REF:-

OUR REF:- WRW:ep

Reply to:

FILM PRODUCTION DIVISION,

Tel. GERRARD 9168/9.

8, Berwick St. W.1.

Kevin Connor Esq.,
Cherry Brow,
Hawkshead Lane,
North Mimms,
Hatfield,
Herts.

Dear Mr. Connor,

   Further to your visit here today, we are
happy to confirm your engagement as Trainee Assistant
Editor at a weekly commencing salary of £4. 10. 0.

   Normal working hours are from 9.30 a.m. to
5.30. p.m. Monday to Friday, but you need not attend
until 10 a.m. on Tuesday the 15th of September.

        Yours sincerely,

        W.R. Weedon.
        Producer.

Courtesy Kevin Connor

Vandyke Picture

CORPORATION LIMITED

DIRECTORS
R. D. PROUDLOCK
D. W. A. BIRTWISTLE
G. J. R. HARRISON
E. LLOYD
P. L. STAFFORD

28 NEW BOND STREET
LONDON, W.1

TELEPHONE
MAYFAIR 1626 (4 LINES)

TELEGRAMS
VANCOR, WESDO, LONDON

CABLES
VANCOR, LONDON

4th. May, 1955.

Kevin Connor Esq.,
Cherry Brow,
Hawkshead Lane,
North Mimms,
Hatfield, Herts.

Dear Mr. Connor,

"THEY CAN'T HANG ME"

This is to confirm your engagement on the above
production in the capacity of 2nd.Assistant Editor, at a
salary of £9.10s. 4d. per week, commencing on 16th. May,
1955.

Yours sincerely,

Ben Arbeid,
Production Manager.

Courtesy Kevin Connor

Alligator named Daisy.

J. ARTHUR RANK PRODUCTIONS LTD.

PINEWOOD STUDIOS
IVER HEATH BUCKS

Jumping for Joy.

TELEPHONE IVER 700

TELE ADDRESS JARPRO, IVER HEATH

YOUR REF
OUR REF /L-W

2nd August, 1955

Kevin G. Connor Esq.,
"Cherry Brow",
Hawkshead Lane,
North Mimms,
Hatfield,
Herts.

Dear Mr. Connor,

This is to confirm your engagement with effect from Tuesday, the 2nd August, 1955, as Second Assistant Editor at Pinewood Studios, at a salary of £10. 0. 0. per week.

The gerenal conditions applicable to your engagement shall be those agreed between the British Film Producers' Association and the A.C.T., as laid down in the National Agreements from time to time, operative between them for employees of your grade.

Membership of the Organisation's Pension Scheme is a condition of employment and when you are eligible full details will be explained to you.

Two weeks' notice is necessary on either side for the termination of your employment.

Yours sincerely,

J. E. FENNELL
Personnel & Studio
Operations Manager

DIRECTORS J ARTHUR RANK, J.P. (CHAIRMAN) SIR MICHAEL BALCON JOHN DAVIS SPENCER M. REIS A. W. ROBINSON EARL ST. JOHN (U.S.A.)

Courtesy Kevin Connor

Top: Pinewood Studios

Bottom: Shepperton Studios mid-60s

Pinewood Studios, Shepperton Studios

Joseph Arthur Rank, or as Connor said, J. Arthur Rank, was a British industrialist and philanthropist who played a significant role in the development of the British film industry. He built his fortune in the aforementioned flour milling business. He transformed his family's small flour mill into a major milling enterprise, eventually founding the Rank Hovis McDougall conglomerate.

As a devout Methodist, Rank also incorporated his strong religious beliefs into his business practices, famously introducing the "Gongman" trademark, which featured a gong being struck by a man in silhouette. His entrepreneurial spirit and passion for filmmaking led him to establish Pinewood Studios, a name that would become synonymous with British cinema.

Pinewood Studios became a hub for film production, offering state-of-the-art facilities and sound stages. The studio's early productions included a variety of films, from dramas to comedies, showcasing the versatility of the space. One of the notable films produced at Pinewood Studios in its early years was *The Lady Vanishes* (1938), directed by Alfred Hitchcock.

It would go on to be home for some of the biggest films ever made including *Superman*, *The Empire Strikes Back*, *The Shining* and a number of James Bond films to name just a few.

"It was a full on studio. Some very nice people. It was a very active studio. It had a plastering department and woodwork shop, two big dubbing stages, and you knew your place and you called everyone 'sir'. You came dressed in a suit and tie. There was no casual dress like there is today."

On arrival in the cutting room block Connor was assigned as a second assistant editor to a comedy film entitled *"An Alligator Named Daisy"* directed by the talented director, J. Lee Thompson. The film was a typical Rank comedy being turned out at the time.

Shepperton Studios was freelance, a different mentality, because you weren't permanently employed. You learned your trade and started to feel your way about—making sound charts and rewinding reels of film. An apprenticeship if you will. At Pinewood it was more of a family company and rank and file organization.

"It was a full-on, very active studio producing its own Rank films. It had a camera department, several large stages, plastering department and woodwork shop, two big dubbing stages, and you knew your place and you called everyone "sir'. You came dressed in a suit and tie. There was no casual dress like there is today.

Pinewood was the real deal but was like going to a public school and getting teased by the established kids. (*"Go to the store and order a box of sprocket holes etc., etc.)* However, it was here I really learned my trade and the 'culture/etiquette' of working in the film industry. It became my second home – so to speak."

He told me that the studio was built around a massive country mansion. At lunchtime he could walk around the grounds in the relaxing atmosphere and could have a picnic lunch. Very different than today, Now it's like Fort Knox."

November 1955, Connor was called-up to serve two years mandatory National Service. The studio offered to delay his entry until the film he was working on (*Jumping for Joy*) was finished, but Connor wanted it out of the way and declined the deferral. 'I wasn't particularly fulfilled working on the mundane comedies being made.'

He did his two years of service bringing him to November 1957. The government had a policy of re-employment meaning that Rank/Pinewood would have to take him back.

Connor wasn't keen on returning to Pinewood and found a job in London working on documentaries and small feature films. But then Pinewood called him, asking him to return on a big comedy film called *Rockets Galore*, as assistant Sound Editor.

By now Pinewood was becoming more of a freelance studio and more diverse films, with interesting subject matter and directors, were being made by outside companies.

During this period, he moved up to first assistant editor position to the iconic editors, Freddy Wilson, Antony Gibbs and Bill Lewthwaite.

By the time the 60s rolled in Connor had also worked for quite a few big time directors (Lindsay Anderson, Karel Reiz, Tony Richardson, Richard Attenborough, Richard Lester, Abraham Polonsky, Michael Cacoyannis) and logged time on large, commercial pictures as Sound Editor.

By the time the 60s rolled in Connor had worked for quite a few important directors (Tony Richardson, Richard Attenborough, Richard Lester and Sandy McKendrick) and logged time on large, commercial pictures as Sound Editor.

The luck of the film industry hit him. "I was working on a picture called *Séance on a Wet Afternoon* produced by Sir Richard Attenborough at Pinewood. He got a call from Attenborough around nine one morning while in the editing studio.

"Oh Kevin, is Derek (the editor) there?" Attenborough asked. Connor hesitated. Derek the editor was *not* there. He was always late, so Connor covered saying the editor had a dental appointment and would be back.

Attenborough continued. "I've been asked by the distributor to take out two minutes from the movie. Do you have any ideas?"

Having viewed the film well over 30 times, Connor knew exactly where two minutes or more could be sliced and no one would ever miss them. He told Attenborough the smart move would to be to lift a single section out instead of going through the film making multiple cuts to get that 30 seconds to a minute and a half out of there.

"Could I see it tomorrow?" Attenborough asked.

"You can see it in an hour if you like, sir." Connor told him.

Connor went to work, winding down the reel on the synchronizer and deleted the scene. He met Attenborough in a screening room with the reel. Attenborough had to ask what was excised and confirmed he never missed what Connor deleted.

1967 (the year I this author born) rolled around and Connor was working as the Sound Editor on 'The Charge of the Light Brigade'(Un-credited on this film - the result of a falling out with the director), he received a call in the cutting rooms from Attenborough asking if he would edit his directorial debut film, Oh! What a Lovely War.

He had never been the sole editor on a film and this was a big musical production for Paramount. The film was based on the play that was very popular at the time. Connor demurred.

"Attenborough persisted, even coming over to the cutting room and singing and explaining the whole film! What a wonderful moment – as you can imagine. Not many directors would do that."

Attenborough had some opposition from Paramount Studios UK execs with Connor being a first time editor, but Attenborough insisted and Connor got the job.

All because Derek the editor had a dental appointment.

FIND THEM AND HANG ON

There were few resources before The Internet, as Kevin Connor attested. I can do the same, and it was on a larger scope than just trying to get college information.

I got most of my early filmmaking knowledge from *Fangoria Magazine*. While most bought it for the gory, bloody stills (The magazine introduced me to Connor's Motel Hell, which drove me to the movies to see it with its bloody pics of the chainsaw-wielding farmer in a pig head and coveralls), I subscribed to it for the articles.

The main thing I learned from the myriad of interviews with horror indie legends-in-the-making like John Carpenter, Tommy Lee Wallace, George Romero, Alan Ormsby, Larry D. Cohen, Frank Henenlotter, Roger Corman (already legendary), and Lloyd Kaufman was: find good people and work with them as long as you can.

I became a professional filmmaker in 2010 with my first feature, *The Fields*, which starred the late Oscar-winner Cloris Leachman and Tara Reid. It was not the film that kicked off working with the same people, but it put me on track.

Making that film was a baptism by fire as it was the first time I produced, believing I was not ready to direct. Being humble threw me into the world of SAG, agents, contract negotiations, celebrity wrangling, location management, public relations, state paperwork, investor negotiations, financing, and so much more.

I produced and wrote *6 Degrees of Hell*, which starred Corey Feldman. This put the pieces together with a cast and crew I would work with over ten years later.

If you look at my *IMDb*, you will see a number of names returning and rolling over from production to production. Faces come and go, and sometimes people go their own ways, but overall, you find great talent in front of and behind the camera, and you "Hang on to them for dear life," as one indie horror filmmaker said in Fangoria decades ago.

When you assemble the right teams, it becomes production shorthand. Where time would be spent conveying a shot to the director of photography or the look of a scene to the art designer, having worked with them previously and multiple times allows a kind of "I got it" before much is spoken.

My directing debut was *Camp Dread* with Eric Roberts, Danielle Harris, and Felissa Rose. There is no doubt Connor's *Motel Hell* had some influence as I borrowed the dark, satirical humor from that film as well as *Psycho II*, which my film owes more to than the *Friday the 13th* splatter flicks.

I rolled a number of cast as well as crew from my *6 Degrees of Hell* into *Camp Dread,* and that made life all the easier. Sitting down with the same director of photography (DP for short) allowed me to know him as well as he got to know me on the previous film. It's also more than just shortcuts in setting up a scene; it's also knowing how your people respond in times of difficulty.

Here's an example.

We had some difficulty with the makeup effects on *Camp Dread.* I won't spill the tea, but to say my director of photography was frustrated with the effects company is putting it mildly. He was spot on with his frustration. He was and is a perfectionist to this day. His work is incredible, and he doesn't just take pride in his cinematography, it defines him as a human being. His work is him and it is inseparable from his identity.

Wojo Photographics, 2013

Wojo Photographics, 2013

Onset of my *Camp Dread* fall, 2013.

Our crew and DP shooting a walking tour of the camp.

Below: The infamous dummy and actors in that scene.

Eric Roberts shows how I felt with that look.

We had a big scene for the finale of the film. One of the main characters is beheaded on the lake's sandy beach in broad daylight with a machete. The effects team hauled out "the gag" (term for special effect). It was a waist-up replica of the actor hooked to a network of hoses that connected to various tanks to pump and spray fake blood for the decapitation.

My DP grew silent and his eyes squinted as he looked at the effect. I read his face, and it showed what I was thinking: The effect looked awful.

It looked like a resuscitation dummy, with its face and head bearing only the simplest resemblance to the flesh and blood actor. The eyes were fake, dead, and lifeless. The skin tone was all off.

If this were a food delivery, I would say, "That's not what I ordered."

This was not the first issue with this effects team, and tensions were running high before this situation. My heart fell. It was an important effect to really deliver the gore to the audience, and I had storyboarded it and went over it in detail when the effects company flew into town six months earlier to make molds and plaster castings of the actors. I was assured it would be exactly what I wanted.

A large chunk of the budget went to the makeup effects, knowing that in these kinds of horror films, the effects often eclipse starshine. The worst insult of all is that the entire crew, the cast (even those not in the scene), and our star, Eric Roberts, were all there to see it in that bright summer sun.

As I stood over the dummy and the effects crew members set up the blood apparatus, oblivious to our clear dismay (or were they ignoring us?), Eric Roberts walked quietly up behind me and whispered into my right ear: "You're being hosed, boss."

I don't know if my DP heard it, but he took that exact moment to walk off the set.

What do you do? You're the director of the film. You wrote this movie. Your cast and an Oscar-nominated celebrity are all standing around looking at you to know your next move. My DP's departure from the set might as well have been casting the first "vote of no confidence" in me as the leader of this production.

Option A is to flip out and rip the effects artist and his crew a new one. It's sometimes called a "bloodletting," and it's public. You go full throttle on the person and destroy them. The problem is, no matter how justified you are, you will never win everyone witnessing. There will always be a percentage who may not side with the offender, but they don't agree with your handling of the situation.

You always lose when you fight a public war.

A star on one of my films once told me that the infamous Christian Bale flap, when he went nuts on the set of *Terminator Salvation* on its DP, was released online by the crew. Crew will only do that when they feel animosity for the person. I was not present for the onset situation, but this star told me that Bale likely deserved the audio leak and that it had been a long time coming.

Did the DP deserve Bale's wrath? It doesn't matter. He chose to declare war on the set, making it his battlefield, and when you do that, the gloves come off and it becomes public domain. Especially in the streaming era.

Option B is I walk off set and suffer quietly. Just walk away. Say nothing. Try to contain your frustration or upset. This might seem the right choice, but it creates a serious vacuum. As the director, if you give up and have no control over this crisis, then who does? You are telling your crew you can't cope with a crisis and then you've earned your votes of no confidence.

I chose Option C. I had over a year-long personal relationship with my director of photography from the previous film and developing this one. I knew his personality, albeit not fully, but well enough to know that his walkout was not personally directed toward me.

He walked away from stress when it became overwhelming for him. In a way, he shuts down when overstimulated. We had a lot of people on set, the sun is always moving, it was an effects shot (which never go easy), and he had a week's history with this effects team that proved difficult from day one.

I knew he believed in me and showed no sign of the contrary. The urge to take this personally and make some public statement demanding he return to set was there. You feel humiliated, embarrassed at the least, and he has his whole crew of assistants, gaffers, and electricians behind him.

No, I was not going to back him into a corner in front of everyone. Even a rabbit will fight if you corner it. I nodded to Eric's words, agreeing, and then walked over to my DP, who was near the back of the boathouse.

Take note he did not "storm off" and was completely gone. His choice to stop about twenty feet away told me that he didn't want to disappear and wanted me to talk to him. Had I stormed off myself, the whole thing would've collapsed.

But I knew him. I knew his work ethic, and I knew this had everything to do with getting the best-looking effect that was worthy of his high standards. He stood silent, taller than me and pensive, a finger to his mouth, biting a nail.

"Did you see that?" He asked me as I drew close. He knew I did. I said so. "I will not shoot that. It looks awful. I won't put my name on something like that."

There it was. It wasn't about not wanting to work for me, or me personally. It was about him and his reputation. I got it.

Fortunately, I was a Monster Kid—one of those kids who ate up the old *Universal* Monsters on Saturday afternoon creature features on TV. I was fascinated with makeup effects and in fourth grade was the only kid to get Dick Smith's how-to makeup book in my class. I read it, used it, and it taught me the fundamentals of makeup special effects.

Fangoria introduced me to Tom Savini, making the legendary makeup artist a star far more important than any movie celebrity. I devoured everything I could on how Savini did his effects as a teenager.

I made my own films all through middle and high school with a silent Super 8mm movie camera. I did my own practical effects work all through the 80s and like Kevin Connor literally cut my film with scissors and joined the cuts with Scotch tape and film cement and a Super 8 cutting block.

"We can do this," I told my DP. He looked at me like I was nuts. His hand went out, pointing the dummy over on the sand and the clueless crew working on it to prep it. His gesture said: "Did you SEE that? How?!"

"Listen," I said calmly. "The main mechanism is in the neck. That's where the blood is rigged to spray. As long as they didn't mess that up, we can save this."

He said nothing. He waited for my solution because so far he wasn't hearing one.

"Go in tight on the neck. Let Nikki bring the blade down and chop the neck. The blood will go and get everything you can but keep it tight like this." I demonstrated with my hands making a makeshift frame. I walked him over to the dummy and knelt.

He followed, the effects crew stepped out of the way. I showed how tight I wanted him to go on the neck...just above the t-shirt collar and just below the chin.

"That doesn't take care of the head and body. You have to see that or the audience won't know what happened." He was so frustrated and refused to make eye contact with any of the effects team.

"Is something wrong?" The lead effects artist looked at both of us, just realizing there was an issue as all of this happened around them. I could see Eric Roberts sitting on a bench at the side of the boathouse in the shadows, watching me with a smile on his face.

He was watching to see how I handled this. It was his first day, and how I handled this would set the tone for the rest of his days on set. This is a guy who's worked with Christopher Nolan and some of the biggest names in the business. His eyes were on me.

"You're right," I said to my DP. I got up and walked him and motioned for the flesh and blood actor to join us. We walked over to the area where he was to meet his gruesome end.

I knelt down on the hot sand and laid out my plan. We would dig a hole in the sand and have the actor lie down on his back, craning his neck backward and down into the hole.

I didn't want to tell my DP how to compose a shot, but for this situation, I told him he would shoot from an angle at the actor's left foot, shooting back in both a wide and then a tight shot. From that forced perspective angle, it would look like his body was headless.

Fake blood would be splashed all around the hole area, and the effects team would bury some pipes and pump blood from the hole, and it would look like a decapitated body.

The actor would provide some nerve-twitched limb action to add some spice to it all.

My DP didn't think it would work, but he didn't refuse. He thought in silence for several minutes, processing the shot in his head. His eyes closed, then opened and closed…then he said in a flat tone, "Let's do it."

Keep in mind, time is money, and the meter is running the whole time we worked through it. The sun is moving, and the light is changing. You're always on a timer. I would say from the time the dummy was brought out to my DP saying "Let's do it," about 20 minutes passed.

Not bad.

We set up the scene and changed the effects plans to the total confusion of the makeup artists. They did as I instructed without knowing why, but they knew enough that I was not happy with the results. Where did the 60 grand on makeup effects go?

The shot worked. The neck bled on cue, he got the right frame capture, and the forced perspective optical illusion worked. See the film for yourself. It wasn't what I wrote, storyboarded, or even wanted, but it came out good nonetheless, and the film was praised by critics for its makeup effects work.

This worked out because I had a crew I knew. I had a director of photography that I knew, and a lot of arguing, mistrust, and wasted time were saved because of this production shorthand.

It wasn't the only incident on that shoot where I had to step in and run special effects defense, but it always worked out because of the solid team I had in place.

A team I knew.

My DP also learned more about me. He gained more confidence in me because I knew my makeup effects and I backed this up several times more. This relaxed him, and he knew he could come to me and express his concerns, and we would work it out.

Time saved.

Money saved.

I will close out this chapter with one more example from Camp Dread. A week later we had a nighttime scene where an actor is strangled to death by barbed wire. The wire slings around a tree and garrotes him, cutting into his neck and bleeding him out as it slices through the flesh and windpipe.

The effect is broken down into three steps:
1. The fake barbed wire slings around the tree and the actor's neck.
2. The fake barbed wire starts the bleeding.
3. The fake barbed wire rips the neck flesh with blood pumping.

The wire was made of thin, gray plastic piping and looked good. The thin piping would be connected to a series of hand pumps that would pipe fake blood from five-gallon buckets up into the small pipe, and the fake blood would come out through all of the spines and barbs on the wire.

The first two steps went off without any problems, and my DP seemed surprised and at ease. So far so good; his body language seemed to say.

The third step entailed the actor to have a fake latex appliance glued to his neck, which was fragile enough that the plastic barbed wire would rip it up and look like shredded flesh.

When the actor came out in front of the crew and my DP, the appliance did not match the rest of his tanned neck skin. It stood out as very white and pale and clearly looked like a piece glued to his throat.

My DP shook his head, threw up his hands, and walked off again to a nearby tree. It was like we were back on the beach a week earlier. This time I walked over and asked what the problem was. It was just he and I, one on one.

"The problem is that doesn't match his skin! It's almost white. The audience can see it isn't his real skin."

I knew that, and I also knew that was okay. "It will work just fine," I assured him.

"How?!" Once again his hand went out like that Picard meme you see where he's exclaiming something and his hand outstretched, usually followed by "What the hell is that?"

I told him that the actor is now bloody from the first two steps. When I call action, he will continue to struggle and shred the latex, and it will mix together in a grisly mess and look absolutely real.

We will get all of that, I told him, and then we will shoot cutaway shots to his feet struggling and kicking up dirt. In the edit, we will cut away from him bleeding and trying to free himself from the wire to his feet. When we cut back to his face, the flesh will be all ripped and mixed with the blood. The pale latex will not be seen. It was simple.

He didn't accept it as easily as last time. He looked at me, and with a clenched jaw said, "I have shot over 400 special effects shots."

"And tonight will be 401," I replied.

HOW IT'S DONE:

The infamous barbed wire shot that went off without a hitch thanks to a terrific crew.

The behind the scenes of how we pulled it off. Knowing the basics of effects works always helps in a pinch.

Wojo Photographics, 2013

Actor Davy Raphaeley plays Vinny in *Camp Dread* and works with the crew to pull the shot off.

I smiled, and he stared at me and relented. He walked back to the camera. We set up the shots, and it all came out great and turned out to be one of the best effects shots in the film.

By knowing him personally and working with him on more than one project, we understood one another better than this all being new to the both of us. His crew knew me, and if my DP said I was okay, then I was okay with them.

I would rank *Camp Dread* up there as one of my favorite shoots despite the challenges, with some being far greater than what I just listed here.

We got through it because we had a top-notch crew and cast, and we knew we were in this for the long haul.

By 1974 Kevin Connor was on his way to finding that dream crew.

THE ROAD TO CAPRONA II

"Let me back-track for a moment," Kevin Connor said to me. "I'd been editing away on various films and getting my breaks with the wonderful Richard Attenborough on *Oh! What a Lovely War, Magic Christian, Young Winston, Romance of A Horse Thief,* but it wasn't enough. "I wanted to do more."

He looked towards producing. "I didn't have a thought about directing," he confided. "That was the big time, you know? It doesn't even cross your mind that you could get into that world." Connor felt that the horror genre—horror films—would be an easy route into producing. He started reading a number of things before coming across a book of short stories, *The* Unbidden, by R. Chetwynd-Haste, who lived in Richmond, not too far from Connor.

"There were about 20 or so of these wonderful short stories. They were fun and they were modern-day. So that was good. It makes things cheaper. I read them all and picked out twelve of them and contacted Hayes. I bought an option on them and I wrote the screenplays with two friends of mine, Robin Clarke and Raymond Christodoulou."

Connor and friends wrote four scripts apiece. He thought they would make for a great TV series and so, with the help of his agent at the time, got the scripts shipped around to various studios but found there was no interest in horror films for television. This was right around 1972-73 when the idea of made-for-TV horror films was something rather alien to executives.

A year later, Milton Subotsky of the renewed Amicus Productions, called and suggested a meeting at Warner Bros HQ in Cork Street, London to discuss the project.

Connor and his agent, John Redway, went to the meeting, and over coffee with Subotsky and the Warner exec, bandied the project back and forth. Milton said he intended to use only four of the stories, that had a common theme, and make them into an anthology feature film. A typical format for Amicus.

"I'll write a connecting story between each of them." Milton said.

He said he would get Peter Cushing to be in it and then out of the blue - " Kevin, you can direct." He offered Connor the directing chores! Just like that! "I nearly fell off my chair," Connor said. " but - but - I've never directed before, Mr. Subotsky" he protested.

Across the pond, however, the Darren McGavin TV vampire in Vegas movie, *The Night Stalker*, was about to change some of that mindset. The scripts did end up on the desk of film producer Milton Subotsky. Subotsky, a name synonymous with imaginative storytelling and genre filmmaking, carved a distinctive path in the world of cinema as a prolific producer and screenwriter, leaving an indelible mark on the landscape of horror, science fiction, and fantasy films.

He was an instrumental figure in bringing the works of iconic authors to the screen and contributed to the evolution of the horror and fantasy genres. His films continue to be celebrated by genre enthusiasts and remain an integral part of the cinematic canon.

Subotsky co-founded *Amicus Productions* with fellow producer Max Rosenberg in the 1960s, becoming a significant player in the realm of genre cinema. Before venturing into filmmaking, Subotsky worked in advertising and publishing, honing his skills in crafting engaging narratives and capturing audiences' attention.

Amicus focused on producing horror, science fiction, and anthology films that captivated audiences with their imaginative and often macabre tales.

Milton Subotsky said he wanted to meet us to talk about the scripts we sent. We went to the *Warner Brothers* lot in London.

Connor and his fellow writers went to the meeting, sat down, and bandied things back and forth with Subotsky, who said he intended to use four of the short stories and make them into an anthology feature film. "I'll write the connecting story between each of them," Milton offered.

He said he could get Peter Cushing to be in it and—he offered Connor the directing chores. Just like that. 'I nearly fell off my chair,' Connor said. 'I've never directed before,' he protested.

He said he could get Peter Cushing to be in it and—he offered Connor the directing chores. Just like that. "I nearly fell off my chair," Connor said. "I've never directed before," he protested.

Subotsky waved that off. "Editors make good directors. They have a sense of when they got it in the can. They don't over cover. They are economical and usually, good directors have come from the cutting rooms." Connor was promised that he would be surrounded by a good crew, good technicians, and would have ample support in his directing debut.

He said if Connor knew of some of his own people that would be fine too. "So how about it?" Subotsky asked.

Connor laughed. "Of course, I said yes."

The film would be an anthology horror called *From Beyond the Grave*, and it was this moment that put Connor on the direct course for Caprona and *The Land That Time Forgot.* "Shepperton Studios was home to Milton and Max's offices, and Connor headed there to helm his first feature film.

The offices were in a wooden hut on the Shepperton Studios back lot. He met much of his future crew that would stay with him on the next several motion pictures.

It was an almost instant family feel, and would yield great results in the subsequent films. "I was allowed to have my own editing and sound crew but not DP, Art Director or Composer. Milton presented me with Alan Hume as DP, Maurice Carter as Art Director but insisted on his regular composer Doug Gamley and casting person. I didn't think it smart to argue at this point – not that I had anyone in mind anyway. The caliber and artistic quality of all these technicians I was presented with was astounding. Not to mention the highly recognizable actors that were assigned to the roles.

"It was London in the '70s," he reminded me. "Really top people across the board wanted to work as employment was low at that time. I would go and meet these actors after they committed and have dinner with them; it was a fantastic experience." Connor had a lot of involvement over the years and had been around film sets, and directing ADR as a Sound Editor, so there was no problem in communicating with actors. However, he had never directed a film or even theater experience.

From Beyond the Grave went into production in May 1973.

The film featured a cast of legendary actors, including Peter Cushing, Ian Bannen, Ian Carmichael, Diana Dors, David Warner, and Donald Pleasence (and his daughter Angela), among others.

"It all becomes your family," Connor said, and I understood what he meant. It was the exact stuff I read so much about as a boy reading Fangoria, and how John Carpenter and George Romero described their sets. Connor would join forces with director of photography Alan Hume, who would go on to lens his next several features. Hume, already a legend, would go on to lens *Return of the Jedi*, several *James Bond* films as well as *Lifeforce* and *A Fish Called Wanda*.

The production shorthand was falling all into place. "You collect your technicians and crew you work with, and life is a little easier. You surround yourself with good people, and we enjoyed making movies.

The whole process was a delight. We always made our days and finished on time. It was such a pleasant experience. However, I had a terrific camera operator, Derek Browne—a top feature operator who had done major films. I didn't have to know too much about lenses or the technical side of the camera, but you do learn and figure out the basic knowledge quickly."

It was Browne, however, who gave Connor advice he would not just take *for Beyond the Grave* but beyond that film to all of his other work. "Always take your camera to the back of the set," Browne told him. "Don't look at it from the front. Look at it from the back. It's always way more interesting. You shoot through things. Always check out the angles from the back of the set. You never know what shots are lurking there."

It was terrific advice on camera setup for shot compositions.

I learned so much from Alan Hume and Derek Browne - where to put the camera, when to track, when to pan and above all – diplomacy with actors. As opposed to American films, on English productions, the director works hand in hand with the camera operator on the setup and camera movements. The DP goes on to work on the overall lighting. You design the track and build it, and you save time because the DP can at the same time fine-tunes his lighting."

Connor went on to describe how American productions differed in that regard. "You come on to American sets, and the operator sits in the corner and reads the paper while the director designs the shot with the DP, who then gets on with the lighting."

From Beyond the Grave was a smooth production and an ideal start for Connor's directing career.

It would put everything in place for him to move right into his next directing feature, which would take him from the graves of England to a lost continent in Antarctica.

It's interesting to note that a number of Connor's cast and crew would go on to work with *Star Wars*, starting in 1977. Peter Cushing, David Prowse would be the big stand outs, but a number of crew and supporting cast members would find their way on Lucas' sets and a few with Lucas and Spielberg.

These people were some of the best and the brightest in the industry and Kevin Connor had them all on his side. *Star Wars* and *Indiana Jones* are grouped with *Superman, James Bond* and even the *Alien* franchises to have Connor's team contribute.

Things like that just don't happen anymore. Not the way it did for Kevin Connor.

Courtesy of Kevin Connor

On set of Connor's directorial debut,

From Beyond the Grave, 1973.

AMICUS PRODUCTIONS LTD.

CALL SHEET

NO. 3

PRODUCTION: "TALES FROM BEYOND THE GRAVE" DATE: Monday, 4th. June, 1973.

STAGE: 1) Old House
2 & 3) 'B' Stage

SETS: 1) INT. LANDING
2) INT. PAMELA'S ROOM
3) INT. EDWARD'S FLAT

UNIT CALL: 8.30am

SCENE NOS: 1) 19a, 21, 23, 24pt, 25 Night
2) 18pt, 19pt Day
3) 3 Night

DIRECTOR: KEVIN CONNOR

Artist	Character	D/R	M/U	ON SET
1) INT. LANDING. Scs. 19a, 21, 23, 24pt, 25 Night:				
DAVID WARNER	EDWARD (V.O.)	44	-	8.30
WENDY ALLNUT	PAMELA	27	7.30	8.30
Stand ins:	For:			
JOHN HAZLETON	Mr. Warner	21	On set	8.30
A.N. Other	Miss Allnut	22	8.00	8.30

PROPS: As per script and breakdown to include Pamela's watch

2) INT. PAMELA'S ROOM. Scs. 18pt, 19pt Day:				
DAVID WARNER	EDWARD (V.O)	44	From above	
WENDY ALLNUT	PAMELA	27	" "	

Stand ins: From above

PROPS: As per script and breakdown to include telephone

3) INT. EDWARD'S FLAT. Sc.3 Night:				
DAVID WARNER	EDWARD	44	From above	
WENDY ALLNUT	PAMELA	27	" "	
JOHN WATTS	JOHN	43	9.00	10.00
HELEN FRASER	MARY	42	9.00	10.00
SCOTT FREDERICK	PETER	41	9.00	10.00
JACQUELINE TONG	HELEN	40	9.00	10.00
MARCEL STEINER	FACE	39	8.00	10.00
Stand ins: For Mr. Warner and Miss Allnut from above, plus:				
DENNIS MARLOWE	For Mr. Steiner	21		10.00

ART/CONSTRUCTION: Prepared mirror, blue mist to pass over surface

PROPS: As per script and breakdown to include drinks, glasses, peanuts, crisps, candle, Pamela's watch.

SP.FX: Candle to fizz and spit flame.

TRANSPORT: Car to pick up Mr. Warner - time to be advised.

Courtesy of Kevin Connor

Courtesy of Kevin Connor

Cinematographer
Alan Hume

Camera Operator
Derek V. Browne

Director KEVIN CONNOR and director of photography ALAN HUME
while shooting ARABIAN ADVENTURE at Pinewood studios

AMICUS

Amicus Productions emerged in the late 1960s as a British film production company

that left an indelible mark on the horror and anthology genres. Founded by Max J. Rosenberg and Milton Subotsky, *Amicus* created a distinct brand of horror cinema that embraced imaginative storytelling and showcased the talents of both established and emerging filmmakers. Let's delve into the formation, films, and inner workings of Amicus Productions during its prominent era in the 1960s and 1970s.

Max J. Rosenberg was a seasoned producer with a passion for storytelling. Rosenberg played a pivotal role in founding Amicus Productions. His vision was to create compelling films that entertained and captivated audiences.

Rosenberg, a prolific producer and visionary figure in the world of cinema, embarked on a career that spanned decades and left a solid mark on the film industry.

Born in Brooklyn, New York, 1914, Rosenberg's career was characterized by a passion for storytelling, a keen eye for talent and new talent with an unwavering commitment to bringing captivating narratives to the silver screen.

His early experiences laid the foundation for his future ventures in the entertainment industry. He displayed an entrepreneurial spirit from a young age, starting a concession business at Coney Island before venturing into the world of film production.

One of Rosenberg's most enduring contributions was the co-founding of *Amicus Productions* in 1962, alongside his creative partner Milton Subotsky.

"Milton was the only creative force of *Amicus*," Connor told me.

The production company gained recognition for its innovative and imaginative approach to horror and fantasy cinema. *Amicus Productions'* motto, "Friend to the Friendly," reflected Rosenberg's dedication to collaboration and camaraderie within the filmmaking community.

Rosenberg's creative vision extended beyond horror and fantasy. He produced a wide array of films (once partnering with the legendary producer Joseph E. Levine) that spanned genres, showcasing his versatility as a producer. From horror anthologies to dramas and comedies, Rosenberg's portfolio reflected his commitment to engaging storytelling.

Rosenberg found himself on the cusp of his first triumph in 1943. With a meager investment of $1,500, he acquired discarded newsreel footage that seemed ready to leave the film can for the garbage can.

Rosenberg meticulously wove together this assortment of seemingly unrelated visuals, birthing a remarkable cinematic creation titled The *Good Old Days*." This compilation of moments captured in time resonated with audiences, becoming an unexpected hit that left its mark on the industry.

As fate would have it, the journey of *The Good Old Days* led Rosenberg down a fortuitous path. It was during the process of presenting this cinematic gem to exhibitors that his path converged with that of a legendary figure, the aforementioned Joseph E.Levine.—a true maverick with a reputation that spanned the cinematic spectrum, Levine was known for his involvement in diverse cinematic ventures, ranging from the grandeur of muscle-bound epics like *Hercules* to the profound subtleties of films like *The Graduate.*

He produced my favorite childhood film, the *Rankin-Bass* stop motion classic, *Mad Monster Party.*

Recognizing the potential of their combined prowess, Rosenberg and Levine forged a partnership that would shape the landscape of film distribution. Together, they established a distribution company that deftly navigated the currents of the cinematic world. Their company took under its wing a range of films, including art-house imports like *The Blue Angel* and the compelling *Open City.*

In this convergence of talent and vision, Rosenberg's journey from salvaging forgotten newsreel footage to becoming a trailblazing force in film distribution took an exhilarating turn. The echoes of his innovative spirit and his collaboration with the enigmatic Levine would leave make its mark with both men laying foundations future filmmakers would build upon.

Time marched on, the paths of Max J. Rosenberg and Joe Levine gradually diverged. Their once harmonious partnership dissipated into the annals of history.

It was not a dramatic parting of ways, marked by clashes or resounding farewells or public nastiness, but rather a subdued farewell that echoed with the hushed weight of unresolved matters.

Rosenberg recalled, "Our partnership ended with a whimper, not a bang, largely because Joe owed me $30,000." That financial reckoning cast its shadow over their shared journey. The grand tapestry of their collaboration had been interwoven with triumphs and challenges, victories and debts, ultimately culminating in a resolution that lacked the flourish of closure.

However, amidst the recollections of financial matters, there remained a remnant of the distinctive Levine touch—a legacy in the form of a peculiar footnote. "Joe's biggest contribution to the film industry was the 28-course meal," muses Rosenberg. That was testament to Levine's penchant for large meals and dining experiences. [1]

Though the partnership had reached its denouement, its imprint endured. As Rosenberg found himself traversing new horizons, the echoes of his past collaborations reverberated in unexpected ways. In the mid-1950s, the cinematic trail led him to the enchanting streets of London, where a fresh chapter awaited. Here, in the heart of a city steeped in history, he would encounter another creative spirit destined to become his partner in artistic exploration—Milton Subotsky.

Rosenberg and Subotsky embraced a high-low road, an approach that seamlessly blended the realms of low-budget horror films with the elegance of more refined cinematic offerings (This will be seen in *The Land That Time Forgot* and its sequel, *The People That Time Forgot*). Their collective vision converged upon the silver screen, crafting a cinematic narrative that danced across the spectrum of genres and experiences.

Amicus' best horror films used the anthology format. Unlike the British *Hammer* label (*Amicus* films were often confused with *Hammer*) in the same era, *Amicus* films were set in the present, not the past, giving them a more modern sensibility.

---

1   *Interview with Max Rosenberg,* Patrick Goldstein, *Los Angeles Times,* August 8, 2003.

They embraced the tropes of swirling mist, haze or fog and people moving through cemetery grounds to that heavy horror music. The fun stuff.

I spent many Saturday afternoons watching these kind of films on local TV syndicate stations like *WPHL 17* out of Philadelphia or *WPIX* Channel 11 out of New York[2]

Rosenberg could squeeze a dollar's worth of production out of a dime. Like Roger Corman and William Castle, he gave a host of young actors their first breaks and had Castle's knack for marketing gimmickry.

Amicus made *City of Dead* (renamed *Horror Hotel* for American theaters) with Rosenberg creating the poster's tag line: "Just Ring for Doom Service."[3]

Rosenberg butted heads with Jack Warner, whose *Warner Brothers* released many of his early films. When Rosenberg pitched the Warner a film about call girls, Warner proclaimed that *Warner Bros.* would never soil its reputation by making a film about pimps and prostitutes.

"Two years later I came back with the same exact story, except I told Jack it was a picture about mental health," Rosenberg recalls. "Jack said go ahead and make it. He had an enthusiasm for filmmaking, but I don't know if that's a virtue or not. I mean, Hitler had an enthusiasm for architecture, didn't he?"[4]

Rosenberg's ability to identify and nurture emerging talent played a pivotal role in his success. He collaborated with a diverse array of filmmakers, writers, and actors, providing them with platforms to showcase their skills and creativity.

---

2   Ibid.
3   Ibid.
4   Ibid.

A young Donald Sutherland got $5,400 for one of his earliest jobs and a free ride to work every morning with Rosenberg. *The Mind of Mr. Soames* has the young Terence Stamp (The future General Zod of *Superman* and *Superman II* fame), while Ian McKellen made his film debut in the 1968 film, *Thank You All Very Much*.[5]

Sarah Douglas, another fresh-faced, young unknown actor would lead *The People That Time Forgot* and would also go on to *Superman* fame as the evil Ursa, General Zod's (Terrance Stamp) partner in Kryptonian crime.

It's no small accomplishment getting 50 films released, nearly all of them made on minuscule budgets. "It was a very frugal operation," says Rosenberg. "I always had to measure what I was getting versus what I was paying. The only perks I ever got were two suits that didn't fit Terence Stamp."[6]

His collaborations with renowned directors like Freddie Francis and Kevin Connor, as well as iconic actors such as Peter Cushing and Christopher Lee, contributed to the unique and compelling nature of *Amicus Productions'* films.

Rosenberg's dedication to innovative storytelling was evident in Amicus Productions' approach to anthology films. These films often featured interconnected stories that captivated audiences and showcased Rosenberg's ability to create narratives that resonated.

Rosenberg's legacy lives on through the enduring impact of Amicus Productions and its contributions to the horror and fantasy genres. The company's films continue to be celebrated by genre enthusiasts and have left an indelible mark on cinematic history.

5   Ibid.
6   Ibid.

Rosenberg's commitment to collaboration, creativity, and imaginative storytelling has inspired filmmakers and audiences alike, solidifying his place as a visionary figure in the world of cinema.

Milton Subotsky was a creative force in his own right, Subotsky's background extended beyond filmmaking, as he had experience in advertising and publishing. His storytelling acumen and entrepreneurial spirit were integral to the company's success. He often wrote or polished scripts for his productions.

He attended the City College of New York, where he honed his writing skills and nurtured his creative passions. Before venturing into the realm of filmmaking, Subotsky embarked on a path in advertising and publishing. These early experiences likely contributed to his ability to craft compelling narratives and capture audiences' attention.

Subotsky would go on to work with huge authors as Stephen King on several film and TV projects (that he bought the rights but never did make. He would have credits on King's *Cat's Eye* and *The Lawnmower Man*).

He worked with talents like director Freddie Francis and actors Peter Cushing and Christopher Lee, forging partnerships that contributed to the success of Amicus films. He also collaborated with the works of other esteemed writers as Edgar Allan Poe, H.P. Lovecraft, and Robert Bloch to the screen, translating their tales into memorable cinematic experiences.

This was an age when imagination still melded with the business end of things to bring interesting and engaging entertainment.

Amicus Productions was officially established in 1962. Rosenberg and Subotsky's shared passion for cinema, especially within the horror and fantasy genres, inspired them to create a platform for filmmakers to explore innovative narratives.

The name *Amicus* was chosen as a tribute to *Amicus Productions'* motto: "Friend to the Friendly." Subotsky was "the artistic one" while Rosenberg was "the money guy" who got the funds.

"Max wasn't around, so to speak." Connor described the two just like this, with Max mostly producing from afar in New York and handing the financial side of things. "Milton loved movies but I didn't get the impression Max LOVED movies. He loved making money."

Connor praised Subotsky as being kind, patient and creative. "He knew what he was doing in making our films. Our budgets were never as big as *Hammer* but Milton wanted to make the best we could. He left me alone and he'd watch the dailies but never interfered or came to set and said "Do this or that." He totally left me alone. I have nothing but love and admiration for him."

Subotsky leaned more toward "family entertainment" which Connor would confirm when it came time for how *The Land That Time Forgot* would take shape. By the time *Amicus* was at *The Land That Time Forgot* stage of their journey, the studio had stumbled a few times in its horror content, with Subotsky being seen as "getting off track" from his instincts.

It seems to make sense that Subotsky did not want an ultraviolent film with *Land* and to keep that family element properly balanced with the horror, scary mix. Their final horror titles would be *The Beast Must Die* in 1974, the same year *Land* released.

Throughout these years the relationship between Rosenberg and Subotsky frayed.

As noted, *Amicus* was known for its anthology films, a format that allowed the company to weave multiple stories within a single film. This approach offered creative freedom, enabling different directors and actors to contribute their unique perspectives to the same project.

The anthology format enabled the company to experiment with diverse narratives, often centered on supernatural or macabre themes. *Dr. Terror's House of Horrors* (1965) and *Tales from the Crypt* (1972) are prime examples of Amicus' successful anthology films.

Amicus cultivated partnerships with esteemed writers and directors, fostering an environment of creativity and collaboration. The company worked with talented individuals such as Freddie Francis, Roy Ward Baker, and of course Kevin Connor, who directed some of *Amicus'* most memorable films and why I centered on him for this book.

The studio produced a roster of iconic films that spanned horror, fantasy, and science fiction genres. Notable titles include *The House That Dripped Blood* (1971 that also put Doug McClure on the company's radar), *"Asylum"* (1972), *From Beyond the Grave* (1974), and *The Land That Time Forgot.*

The company's films often featured tales of suspense, the supernatural and psychological intrigue, attracting audiences seeking imaginative and captivating storytelling.

Amicus carved a unique niche in the horror genre, distinguishing itself through its anthology format and commitment to engaging narratives. The company's films continue to be celebrated by genre enthusiasts and filmmakers.

While *Amicus* ceased operations in the late 1970s, its legacy endures as a testament to the creative spirit of independent filmmaking and the ability to craft memorable stories that transcend time.

Amicus Productions' legacy is one of creative exploration, innovation, and dedication to bringing captivating tales to the silver screen. The company's films remain a cherished part of horror cinema history, captivating audiences with their imaginative narratives and timeless appeal.

I went back into the company's catalogues thanks to *Tubi* and watched more than just Connor's films to see the evolution firsthand. I left wishing I was making films during that era. While the corporate mindset was always there, and there really are no "good old days", there was a more lenient kind of way to filmmaking it appears.

In the case of *Amicus* it seemed there was more attention to cultivating real talent, utilizing resources to their potentials. The company trusted its filmmakers—allowing them to assemble their own crews, make their own decisions, without the heavy-handed oversight witnessed today and in recent decades.

The executive stranglehold over creativity which messed with such films as The Exorcist III and Alien 3 was not that way with Subotsky and Rosenberg. I saw something similar in the making of 1977's *The Last Dinosaur* where producers Arthur Rankin and Jules Bass were allowed free hands to make the movies and projects they wished to make.

"They had a pedigree," producer Benni Korzen told me. "They had a track record." He went on to describe Rankin and Bass as laid back and hands off. They knew how to get shit done.

This appears to be the case with Rosenberg and Subotsky, who also cultivated new talent and embraced the old as well. Their "high concept, low budget" style served them well and it is still clear today when re-watching *Horror Hotel* which was nicely shot, well edited and put together.

They had plenty of William Castle in their work, but they also had a healthy dose of *Hammer* and high concept to go along with it. They deviated in quality over the years but what studio hasn't?

Subotsky's influence would also be seen with Kevin Connor, not just on the his giant monster pictures, but *Motel Hell*. Whether consciously or not, the film came across to me as a boy as ultra bloody and violent.

A recent viewing (even though I have seen it several times on video since 1980) showed me through the eyes of a professional filmmaker, that the film, much like its 1974 inspiration, *The Texas Chainsaw Massacre*, is rather tame in its helpings of blood and gore.

Much of the horror is implied and when the horrific moments come, the ones that stayed in my head when I went to sleep contained zero blood and gore or even chainsaws.

I will get into great detail on that aspect in the volume on Connor's *Motel Hell*.

Amicus would have a good run and throughout this history of Connor's work, we will look into the causes of its eventual demise. Connor attributes some of that to the arrival of John Dark within the company and the tensions that would bring with Subotsky.

"There was an animosity, but basically they didn't like each other. Subotsky felt Dark wasn't needed and Dark was a drain of money. Max wanted him, however."

The company would become entwined with American schlock producer Samuel Z. Arkoff of *American International Pictures* right around the time of *The Land That Time Forgot*.

One thing I do know is that my childhood and career are far richer because *Amicus* was in my young adult world.

Max J. Rosenberg and Milton Subotsky

Courtesy of Tane McClure Arendts

L-R (Back): John Dark, Kevin Connor, 1st AD Brian Coates
Front: DP Alan Hume (front)

Courtesy of Tane McClure Arendts

L-R : Kevin Connor, Doug McClure, Jack Holland, John Dark

CHARTING COURSE

Tales From Beyond the Grave didn't do great but it did well enough. Warner Bros., the American distributor didn't really get behind it. As a filmmaker I have always wondered why major studios do this. They put money into a film, whether to make it or release or both, and then suddenly leave it almost fend for itself or put the bare minimum into the release.

There are two horror films that come to mind as we move toward *The Land That Time Forgot*. The first would be *Halloween III*, the 1982 "sequel that wasn't a sequel" installment into the slasher franchise that is not part of the franchise. Makes sense? No? Well it didn't to me either when I saw the film opening weekend and then recently collaborated on a book about its making with its director and writer, Tommy Lee Wallace.

The short version is Wallace and company turned in a film that had absolutely nothing to do with the original 1978 film and its 1981 sequel. Universal Studios still called it *Halloween III* but its subtitle *Season of the Witch* was its true and only title.

Wallace had no interest in making a third "Haddonfield" *Halloween* film and even walked away from the 1981 *Halloween II* even with it being a guaranteed success. It was a gun for hire job and he felt there was no more story to tell after the 1978 original.

He felt even more so when approached to make *Halloween III*. Admitting he might've hobbled his own career by turning down *Halloween II* he agreed to *Halloween III* but wanted the guarantee that the film would have zero to do with the previous two films.

The goal was to create a whole new franchise, basically a new Halloween-holiday movie each year with a different story in the vein of an anthology or series. Universal knew this. They green lit the project knowing full well it would have nothing to do with the previous two films.

"The Shape," Tommy referred to Michael Myers' nickname, "was dead." There was nothing else to the story.

When the final film was handed in, Universal turned an indifferent position and threw it out into the public without a solid marketing plan. They didn't say it was a true sequel to *Halloween*, knowing audiences would think that with the ham-fisted *Halloween III* as the main title; but they didn't deny it either.

"They weren't behind it," Tommy told me. "They just went through the motions in releasing it and the results were not surprising."

The backlash was swift and venomous and for decades *Halloween III: Season of the Witch* held the dubious title of most despised sequel in the franchise.

The irony is that it was never to be a sequel and the suits at Universal just didn't care.

The best Universal did was slap "All New!" on the posters. Tommy asked just what the hell that meant. It sounded like a toothpaste ad. Universal would do the same thing a year later with *Jaws 3-D*, slapping "All New!" on that poster art as well.

The studio would do it again on the 1982 release of John Carpenter's *The Thing*. Once *ET: The Extraterrestrial* smashed all box-office records, the studio just kind of let "the other alien movie" to die in the cold.

There was little marketing for the film and they packaged it as a remake to the Howard Hawks '50s era sci-fi classic (which gets some love in Carpenter's original *Halloween*).

The film really wasn't a remake and if anyone went into the theater thinking it was, they found that the film veered way off from the original. Instead it was more of a direct translation of the original novella source material, *Who Goes There?*

Instead of a giant, hulking humanoid alien menace, we got this gooey, shape shifting cellular organism that could take the shape of any living thing it touches. It was a big bait and switch and the movie died but its alien would not resurrect like *ET* for another 30 years as time rehabilitated what may be Carpenter's greatest film and one of the best horror films ever made.

Third time is a charm with Universal and they did the same thing to 2011's *The Thing*—a PREQUEL to the 1982 Carpenter film, but the lack of marketing and studio support allowed audiences to think we were getting a remake to Carpenter's original.

The studio left it for dead and the film flopped. To make matters worse the practical effects (which defined the 1982 film) were all replaced by CGI and the ending was changed. Universal washed their hands of a project that never got a fair shake from its inception.

Did Warner's go that far with *From Beyond the Grave*? Not exactly, but the budgets were different. Connor felt it didn't give him the big boost in his career he had hoped. While it got some decent reviews, he recalled one critic who described his directing style as having all the grace of a cement truck.

"I got an interview with the *BBC*," he admitted, but *From Beyond the Grave* did not do a lot for him. It didn't help that a powerful studio like Warner's just gave it the bare minimum in its release.

Like the films I mentioned before it, *From Beyond the Grave* would find a new life beyond the film grave in the home video and TV world; earning a respectable cult following over the subsequent decades.

The film did open the doors to *The Land That Time Forgot* and the pathway for the success Connor hoped for.

From Beyond the Grave did perform and it did well enough for Subotsky to come back to Connor with the offer to direct a larger picture action film based on an Edgar Rice Burroughs property.

"They came to me after that and said, we'd like you to do this much bigger picture for us. It's a quarter of a million dollars budget. It was a lot of money for them and a lot of money for all the special effects involved.

They'd been working on it while I was working of *Tales*. They had ideas on how to do things, do them cheaply. It was already in development by the time they came to me."

The Land That Time Forgot was initially serialized in the pages of "Blue Book Magazine" in 1918 before being published as a novel later that year. Its imaginative depiction of a lost world filled with dinosaurs captured the imagination of readers, drawing them into a realm where the past coexisted with the present.

While Burroughs is perhaps best known for his creation of iconic characters like *Tarzan* and *John Carter of Mars*, *The Land That Time Forgot* was a beloved and enduring work in the realm of science fiction literature.

The book caught the attention of Milton Subotsky who read it and contracted two writers, John Moorcock, a prolific British author known for his contributions to the fantasy and science fiction genres.

Moorcock's task involved condensing the rich narrative of the novel into a coherent and engaging screenplay while retaining its core elements. The story follows a group of World War I survivors who find themselves stranded on a mysterious and dangerous prehistoric island.

James Cawthorn was a British artist, writer and received a screenwriting credit alongside Moorcock. His partnership with Moorcock extended beyond just writing; they often worked together on literary and artistic endeavors, contributing to each other's projects. In the case of *The Land That Time Forgot,* Cawthorn's background in both illustration and writing likely influenced the visual and narrative aspects of the screenplay.

Before the script landed into the hands of Kevin Connor, Subotsky took a writing pass; streamlining certain things but being a writer himself, made sure the film adaptation followed the central concept of the book. Subotsky wanted to stay as loyal to Burroughs' work, likely because it had such a following and the writer in him might see it as an affront to a legendary author.

Subotsky offered the directing chores to Connor who accepted by calling that simple process, "Lovely." Just like that he landed his second feature directing gig and it was total change of genre and a bigger film.

"The script was very good and I enjoyed it. I could see it in my head, and knew what to do. The same crew and team that worked with me on *From Beyond the Grave* would return for *Land*."

The big question was about the big reptiles. Just how were they going to be done? This was a big screen dinosaur action film and there were only several options in 1973 for creating giant monsters on film.

DINO EFFECTS

Filmmakers had the following options to bring their giant monsters to life:

"Suitmation," also known as "suitmation" or "man-in-suit," is a practical special effects technique used to bring monsters, creatures, and other fantastical beings to life on the screen. This method involves a performer wearing a costume or suit designed to resemble the desired creature. The actor inside the suit performs the movements and actions of the creature, while the suit itself is often intricately designed and operated to create the illusion of a living entity.

Key Elements of the Suitmation Process:

Creature Design: The process begins with the creation of a detailed creature design by

special effects artists and designers. This design takes into account the creature's appearance, size, movement capabilities, and any unique features or abilities it possesses.

Construction of the Suit: The creature suit is meticulously crafted to match the design, using materials such as foam, latex, rubber, and various textiles. The suit incorporates mechanisms for movement, such as joints, levers, and cables, to allow the performer to manipulate the creature's motions.

Performers: Skilled actors are chosen to portray the creatures inside the suits.

These performers must be physically adept and capable of conveying emotions and movements that suit the creature's characteristics.

Filming Techniques: Filming suitmation sequences requires careful coordination between the performer inside the suit, the director, and the camera crew. To create the illusion of a larger-than-life creature, filmmakers often use specific camera angles, lighting, and perspectives.

Interaction with Other Actors and Sets: When the creature interacts with other actors or objects in the scene, the suit performer must synchronize their movements to maintain the illusion of realism. This often involves rehearsing and choreographing the actions.

Examples of Suitmation in Films:

Godzilla **Series:** The iconic Godzilla franchise is perhaps one of the most well-known examples of suitmation. Actors don elaborate suits to portray the towering Godzilla and other kaiju creatures. The suits are designed with movable parts for the monster's iconic roars, tail swipes, and destructive actions.

Ultraman **Series:** In this Japanese sci-fi series, the titular superhero battles various giant monsters. The monsters are portrayed through suitmation, with actors inside suits engaging in combat scenes with the hero.

Gamera **Series:** Similar to Godzilla, the Gamera series features a giant turtle monster and his enemies portrayed through suitmation.

King Kong (1976) **and** *King Kong Lives* **(1986):** "Man in Monkey Suit" Rick Baker advanced the suitmation process and took an Academy Award for his efforts as Kong was a live action performer the second time around instead of a stop-motion model. The evolution would continue from suitmation to full CGI in the coming *Monsterverse* series kicked off by 2014's *Godzilla* and then *Kong Skull Island* and *Godzilla vs. Kong*.

"**Stop Motion Animation**" is a meticulous, expensive and time-consuming technique used to bring creatures, dinosaurs, and other objects to life on screen. It involves capturing a series of individual frames, with slight adjustments to the position of the subject between each frame. When played in sequence, these frames create the illusion of movement.

This process allows filmmakers to achieve realistic and fluid motion for creatures that would be challenging to portray using other methods.

The pioneer of this process was Willis O'Brien, the artists behind the original (and first big monster tramples city film) *The Lost World* in 1925 and then on to *King Kong* (1933), and *Son of Kong*. O'Brien launched the process in 1915's *The Dinosaur and the Missing Link*.

O'Brien's protégé, Ray Harryhausen will carry the torch, taking the process even further to create classics and almost the whole sci-fi genre of the 1950s. Their work can't be underestimated and Harryhausen's artistry with dinosaurs eclipsed mentor O'Brien as film went to color. *The Valley of Gwangi* (Basically *King Kong* with a T-rex instead of an ape), *One Million Years B.C., It Came From Beneath the Sea, 20 Million Miles to Earth* and countless others made the Oscar-winning Harryhausen inseparable from the history of stop motion visual effects and paved the way for the modern CGI process.

Key Elements of Stop Motion Animation:

Armature Construction: An armature, or internal skeleton, is constructed to provide a framework for the character or creature. This armature allows for precise positioning and movement of the model's limbs and body parts.

Model Creation: The character or creature is sculpted or built around the armature, using materials such as clay, foam, latex, or plastic. The level of detail in the model contributes to the final realism of the animation.

Set Design: Detailed miniature sets and props are created to provide a backdrop for the animation. These sets need to be carefully designed to scale and can range from lush landscapes to urban environments.

Lighting and Photography: Proper lighting is crucial for achieving consistent and realistic results. Each frame is meticulously photographed, often using a technique called stop motion capture, where the camera is triggered remotely.

Frame-by-Frame Animation: The animator moves the model slightly between each frame while referring to a storyboard or script. This process is repeated hundreds or even thousands of times to create fluid motion.

Post-Production: After capturing all the frames, they are edited together to create the final animation sequence. Sound effects, music, and additional visual effects may be added to enhance the scene.

Using real, living reptiles to create dinosaur special effects in motion pictures was a technique employed since the early days of cinema. It was also my least favorite of the dinosaur razzle dazzle as a boy.

While it gets points for being inventive, the problem is familiarity. Even as a kid you knew the dinosaurs were big flesh and blood lizards (usually Monitor lizards, iguanas and alligators) with plastic fins glued to them. There was nothing "fantastic" about them. When you hear "dinosaur movie" you want T-rex, Stegosaurus,

Triceratops, not your friend's Bearded Dragon running around a fake jungle.

I'm not saying the kaiju in *Godzilla* movies came anywhere close to real, but it was the *surreal*--the out of this world designs of the creatures and the inventiveness of some of the suits that captivated me. The same for stop motion monsters. They didn't move naturally, they looked animated but it didn't matter. I was glued to the TV.

Suspension of disbelief was key in those effects because they were delivering something different—something that didn't exist any longer. It was special.

This is why the limitations of "Suitmation" left me under-whelmed in 1976's *King Kong* because there were no other mon-sters for Kong to fight aside from that dopey rubber snake. They might've been better off using a real anaconda for that scene.

Less than two years earlier I sat transfixed in the theater with *The Land That Time Forgot* because it threw dinosaurs at me left and right. I was a dino junkie and I got my fix.

Kong '76 left me shrugging and feeling it was just okay.

The "real lizards in drag" approach, referred to as "realism through substitution," aimed to bring authenticity to prehistoric creatures by using actual animals. While I guess this method had its advantages, it also posed significant challenges and ethical consid-erations. It also seemed a little lazy.

Challenges and Considerations:

Limited Movement: While using live reptiles provided a certain level of realism, these animals often had restricted movement and behavior that did not match the intended actions of the dinosaurs.

Ethical Concerns: The use of live animals raised ethical concerns, as the animals could be subjected to stress, harm, or discomfort during filming. *PETA* would have a field day with this if it was still used.

Scale Mismatch: Many reptiles used were significantly smaller than the intended dinosaurs, requiring creative camera angles and forced perspective to make them appear larger.

This leads us to the style Kevin Connor went with in *The Land That Time Forgot* and why the film made such an impression on me the first time I saw it as a kid.

Connor and his team (led by Roger Dicken) looked at all of the styles listed above to do their dinosaur effects. They settled on a lesser used technique of actual hand puppets. "They were kind of like Muppets," Connor recalled. "They were also highly detailed and that is what impressed me."

Connor's films (*Land* and *People That Time Forgot*) used a combination of techniques to create realistic and interactive prehistoric animals. It was done through the following techniques:

Animatronics and Puppetry:

Mechanical Creatures: Skilled animators and puppeteers crafted mechanical puppets and animatronic models to simulate the movements and behaviors of dinosaurs. These puppets were often constructed with articulated joints and controlled remotely by puppeteers, allowing for precise and controlled motions.

Cable-Controlled Puppets: Some scenes featured cable-controlled puppets suspended from above, enabling them to move realistically within the environment. Puppeteers would manipulate the cables to create lifelike actions, such as walking or attacking.

Hybrid Approaches: These films used a combination of these techniques, including hand-operated puppets, rod puppetry, and cable controls. Puppeteers would work in coordination to bring different parts of the creature to life, such as the head, limbs, and tail.

Interactive Performances: Puppeteers often collaborated with actors on set to create seamless interactions between human characters and the puppet creatures. This required precise coordination and timing to make the interactions convincing.

Realism and Artistry: The goal of the puppetry style was to achieve a sense of realism and immersion. Skilled puppeteers focused on mimicking natural movements and behaviors, ensuring that the creatures appeared to respond to their environment and the characters around them.

The Land That Time Forgot used a variety of practical effects, including animatronic puppets and puppetry, to depict dinosaurs such as the iconic Mosasaurus. The creature's movements, including its attack scenes, were likely achieved through a combination of mechanical puppetry and cable controls.

I will get to that attack scene in detail as we move through the film and analyze key scenes. I can say *The Land That Time Forgot's* Mosasaurus scene gave me far better thrills the first time I saw it than the one in *Jurassic World*. Sure, I was seven, but that seven-year-old was still in me viewing the Spielberg franchise film that opening weekend, (in 3-D no less) and I was left feeling "Been there, done that."

The trick that Kevin Connor pulled off was making me leave the theater with a "How'd they do that?" sense of wonder. These days we all know how. Thanks to the excessive coverage of DVD extras and The Internet, the magicians no longer have secrets.

We know now how they do it and it's computers.

Whereas Connor's film has a small cadre of effects artists in the end credits the new *Jurassic* films or any *Star Wars*, comic book film of your choice has blocks of artists that go one for much of the end credit scroll dedicated to just digital effects work.

"When I first saw *Jurassic Park* and they panned up to that giant dinosaur, and we all saw it for the first time, I went "Oh shit! Why didn't I have these effects then! Oh bloody hell why didn't we have the money or the technology to that in England back then?"

Connor laughed at the spectacle of it all. "It was pretty mind-bending and awe-inspiring because we had people operating these puppets with hands up their bums.

How could we compete with *Jurassic Park*?"

Then Connor graciously summed it up by saying, "We took the torch from Ray Harryhausen and ran with it for a few more years. Our producer John Dark worked with Harryhausen on *Jason and the Argonauts* (which netted Harryhausen an Oscar)."

Connor got to meet Harryhausen and said the effects wizard was "very complimentary" on *The Land That Time Forgot's* visual effects. "We had good old chat about things," he said. "A lovely man."

I told Connor that I feel this was the era where I should've made movies.

"I know what you mean," he told me. "There was no green screen, blue screen, stuff like that. They rolled out gravel, built pathways for the dinosaurs. They made real fire and brimstone and to this day I am still not sure how they did it all but it was brilliant."

MGM Studios

MGM Studios

MGM Studios

MGM Studios

Modelshipsinthecinema.com

MGM Studios

Special Effects artist, Roger Dicken with just some of his creatures for Kevin Connor.

VISUAL EFFECTS

Visual Effects by Cliff Culley resulted in some
terrific matte paintings and artistic style.

Sets and discussions were already underway when Kevin Connor
was brought on to *The Land That Time Forgot*. While the film's lead
star was already cast, Connor insisted on many of the previous team
from *Beyond The Grave*; including his cutting room team lead by
John Ireland.

"Everybody else in cast, aside from Doug McClure had a say. We
had a wonderful casting person [missing from opening and closing
film titles], who came up with some really great ideas. A lot of the
actors I knew were stage actors and had seen them around and in
other films.

John McEnery and Susan Penhaligon, Keith Barron, were new
acquaintances and Anthony Ainley I worked with, so I put forward
a number of these actors from having worked with them as a sound

editor. I did ADR and got to know a lot of them or was fond of and suggested them for the film."

Connor never had a problem if there was someone he wanted. "As long as they weren't an alcoholic or whatever, I was given a free hand in casting and crew."

"I got to know a lot of the young actors with working on *Oh, What a Lovely War*. So I used a lot of them with this film. There was no "You gotta have this one or that one."

Amicus was terrific on the staffing front. "No complaints whatsoever."

Having almost twenty years in the industry with a body of experiences paid off for Connor. He had come across talent in front and behind the camera and when finally poised for the top role as director, was able to draw upon all of it with solid results.

"It's a team effort," Connor affirmed. "I wasn't Spielberg. I got a break."

Before getting into the casting of Doug McClure, it's important to point out the crew and the main crew chiefs that would set the tone, feel and look of the film.

This was a unique time in film history. The global economy was taking the hit of the burgeoning energy crisis and growing economic downturns. The film industry was hit hard and the downside to that is people were out of work and had bills to pay.

The upside was the availability of top end people for lower budgeted films because people just want to work. This went for both cast and crew. Connor was in the same boat—just happy to have a job and one that entailed dinosaurs.

"There was a wonderful guy at Pinewood Studios named Charlie Staffell who was in charge of all the back projection and front projection—he was the Go to Guy. It's the quality of the plates that matters in front projection."

Staffell would helm the visual plates for *The Land That Time Forgot*. He held various positions in the film industry, including back projection, process photography, optical effects, and projection.

His notable contributions span from 1942 to 1993. His career began as a special effects camera assistant on the film *In Which We Serve* (1942), co-directed by Noel Coward and David Lean, with cinematography by Ronald Neame BSC. He honed his expertise in back projection, contributing to films like *This Happy Breed* (1944), Olivier's rendition of *Henry V*, *Brief Encounter*, and extending all the way to *2001: A Space Odyssey*, *Live and Let Die*, and *Octopussy*.

Staffell had his name on other huge films as *Superman* (1978), *Dune* (1984) and *Aliens* (1986).

Staffelll was honored with an Academy Award of Merit in 1969 for pioneering the successful implementation of the reflex background projection system for composite cinematography.

In 1988, Staffelll's exceptional talents were acknowledged with a Primetime Emmy Award for Outstanding Achievement in Special Visual Effects. This recognition came for his contributions to the television mini-series *War and Remembrance* (1988), directed by Dan Curtis and lensed by Dietrich Lohmann.

A lasting tribute to his legacy, Staffelll posthumously received the BSC's Bert Easey Technical Award in 2000. This esteemed accolade was bestowed upon him in recognition of his invaluable contributions and innovations that have greatly enriched the realm of visual effects.

It's here where a moment should be taken to break down the front and rear projection process since the visual effects were a key component to the success of *The Land That Time Forgot* and just why Staffell was integral to film.

Front Projection is a technique used in visual special effects to combine two separate elements into a single shot. It involves projecting an image or scene onto a screen positioned between the camera and the subject. Here's a breakdown of the front projection process:

Setup: A camera is placed in front of a screen, typically a semi-reflective material, which can reflect light back towards the camera. The subject, such as actors or objects, is positioned between the camera and the screen.

Projection: An image or background scene is projected onto the screen from behind the camera. This image is aligned with the camera's perspective and the movements of the subjects.

Capture: The camera records both the projected image on the screen and the live-action subjects in the foreground in a single shot. The reflective properties of the screen help blend the projected image with the subjects, making them appear as if they are in the projected environment.

Benefits: Front projection can create realistic and convincing scenes where the subjects appear to be interacting with the projected environment. It is often used for scenes that require characters to appear in locations that are impractical or impossible to shoot on location.

Challenges: Front projection may require careful lighting and calibration to ensure the projected image integrates seamlessly with the live-action subjects. Additionally, the screen's reflective properties can sometimes cause unwanted reflections or hotspots.

Rear projection is another technique used in visual special effects to combine elements. It involves projecting an image or scene onto a screen placed behind the subject or actors. Here's a breakdown of the rear projection process:

Setup: A screen is positioned behind the subjects, and a camera is placed in front of them. The subjects are positioned between the camera and the rear projection screen.

Projection: An image or background scene is projected onto the rear screen from behind the subjects. The projected image is aligned with the camera's perspective and the movements of the subjects.

Capture: The camera records both the live-action subjects in the foreground and the projected image on the rear screen. This creates the illusion that the subjects are interacting with the projected environment.

Benefits: Rear projection can be used to place subjects in realistic or imaginary settings. It is often employed when shooting on location is not feasible, and it allows for greater control over lighting and camera movements.

Challenges: Proper lighting and calibration are essential to ensure that the subjects and the projected images appear cohesive. Care must be taken to avoid shadows cast by the subjects onto the rear screen.

All of this goes hand in hand with director of photography whose job is to get the shots by shooting "plates" for the visual effects for either front or back projection.

"Plates" in the context of visual effects refer to background or foreground elements that are separately filmed to be combined with other footage during post-production. Plates serve as the foundation upon which various visual effects are added to create a seamless final composite. This process is often used in conjunction with front and back projection techniques. Here's how shooting plates works:

Front Projection Plates:

Background Plate: In front projection, the background plate is the scene or environment that will be projected onto the screen behind the subjects. To shoot the background plate, the camera is set up in the desired location and records the scene without any actors or foreground elements.

Foreground Plate: The foreground plate is the live-action footage of the subjects or actors that will be filmed against the front projection screen. The camera captures the subjects in a way that aligns with the projected background.

Projection and Recording: During filming, the projected background is displayed on the front projection screen while the camera captures both the foreground subjects and the projected background. The screen's reflective properties help integrate the two elements.

Composite: In post-production, the foreground plate and the background plate are combined using various techniques, such as layering and masking. The projected background becomes the backdrop against which the live-action subjects are placed, creating the illusion of interaction with the environment.

Back Projection Plates:

Foreground Plate: For back projection, the foreground plate involves filming the live-action subjects or actors against a semi-transparent screen. The subjects are placed between the camera and the screen.

Background Plate: The background plate is a pre-recorded scene or image that will be projected onto the rear screen. This scene is aligned with the camera's perspective and the movements of the subjects.

Projection and Recording: The projected background is displayed on the rear screen, and the camera captures both the live-action subjects and the projected background. The screen's semi-transparency allows the subjects to be filmed in front of the projected scene.

Composite: During post-production, the foreground plate and the background plate are combined. The projected background becomes the backdrop behind the subjects, creating the illusion of them being in the projected environment.

Benefits and Challenges:

Benefits: Shooting plates for visual effects provides flexibility and control over the final composite. Filmmakers can create realistic scenes that would be difficult or costly to achieve on location. This process also allows for precise alignment between live-action elements and projected backgrounds.

Challenges: Proper lighting, perspective, and synchronization are essential to ensure that the subjects and the projected elements appear natural and cohesive. Care must be taken to avoid shadows, reflections, and other inconsistencies that could disrupt the illusion.

Throughout both the front and back projection processes, the DP and VFX artists maintain a collaborative relationship. They communicate effectively to achieve the desired visual effect, addressing challenges and making necessary adjustments to create a cohesive and convincing final composite. The DP's expertise in lighting, camera placement, and visual aesthetics is essential to ensure that the live-action and projected elements blend seamlessly, resulting in a visually impressive and engaging scene.

All of this has now changed with the advent of Blue Screen and now Green processes and the advances in digital compositing. Shooting plates for digital post work is similar in theory but very different in post production practice.

Front Projection Process:

Pre-Production Collaboration:

The DP collaborates with the VFX team to discuss the intended visual effects and the background scenes to be projected. They work together to plan the lighting and camera setup, ensuring that the live-action subjects are lit and positioned correctly to match the projected background.

On-Set Coordination:

The DP ensures that the front projection screen is positioned correctly and the projector is aligned accurately with the camera's perspective. They work closely with the camera operators to capture shots that seamlessly integrate the live-action subjects and the projected background.

Lighting adjustments are made to ensure that the subjects are properly lit and match the lighting conditions of the projected scene.

Communication and Feedback:

The DP maintains open communication with the VFX team during filming to address any issues or adjustments needed to achieve the desired visual effect. They provide feedback on the integration of live-action and projected elements, ensuring that the composition, lighting, and perspective match convincingly.

Back Projection Process:

Pre-Production Planning:

The DP collaborates with the VFX team to plan the background scenes that will be projected onto the rear screen. They work together to ensure that the live-action subjects are appropriately placed and lit to match the projected background.

On-Set Execution:

The DP oversees the lighting setup to minimize shadows and ensure proper illumination of both the subjects and the rear projection screen. They work closely with the camera crew to capture shots that effectively integrate the live-action subjects and the projected background.

Real-Time Adjustments:

The DP may make adjustments to the lighting and camera setup based on real-time feedback from the VFX team to ensure seamless integration during filming. They collaborate with the VFX team to address any challenges that arise, such as reflections or lighting inconsistencies.

Post-Production Collaboration:

After filming, the DP works closely with the VFX artists during the post-production process.

They provide input on color correction, grading, and other visual adjustments to enhance the integration of the live-action and projected elements.

Alan Hume was the director of photography on *The Land That Time Forgot*. Hume carried over with Connor from *Beyond the Grave*. "I knew Alan because he was a regular DP at Pinewood and Shepperton. You get to know them at the canteens, the bars and pubs. You form friendships and bonds and it translates well onto the set."

It was Hume who came up with the idea of shooting the visual effects plates on *VistaVision*. This was a widescreen film format developed by Paramount Pictures in the 1950s. It was designed to address some of the limitations of the standard 35mm film format and provide higher image quality and resolution. *VistaVision* utilized 35mm film stock, but it was oriented horizontally rather than vertically, which allowed for larger individual film frames.

"It was a double-sized negative," Connor said. "So when you project it, the quality of it was superb. You could enhance the detail of the dinosaurs."

Hume tracked down a guy at *Technicolor* who had a handheld VistaVision camera that took two-hundred foot rolls. They leased the camera and integrated into the visual effects department. This would allow better looking monsters that brought out the best of what the puppetry offered.

The "Production Shorthand" I spoke of earlier was already in motion which allowed the film to move efficiently through pre-production with a crew that worked like well-oiled machinery.

The film boasted innovative matte paintings that resulted in a
unique consistency in art direction and vision for
The Land That Time Forgot.

MGM Studios

DOUG McCLURE

Doug McClure found himself impersonated on *The Simpsons* at one point and had to ask his daughter if it was tribute or were they making fun of him? He was portrayed as "Troy McClure" a "washed up actor" who was a combo between Doug and Troy Donahue.

McClure came around to find the homage funny and his own daughters would call him "Troy McClure" getting in on the joke. His sense of humor toward this satire shows the kind of guy Doug McClure was.

He never broke into feature films as an A-list actor. The entertainment gods, for whatever reasons, felt his home was television. We get to see what could've been in Kevin Connor's films. There's a great action hero there and someone who could've easily paired alongside Harrison Ford in the *Indiana Jones* films as a terrific side-kick, best buddy.

Opportunity missed, Spielberg.

By many accounts he was a farm boy, living rural in Glendale, California and learning how to get his hands dirty and rope and ride horses by eight years of age. No surprise he was the high school quarterback and you can envision him charming the cheerleaders with the rugged leading man good looks and tough guy persona so well crafted onscreen.

He graduated to study acting, ending up and The University of California, Los Angeles where got into modeling and TV commercials.

He started doing features, mostly as supporting roles, but was creating an image as a Western tough guy and cowboy. This opened the door to TV episodes where that persona took in the McClure image that went out to America.

Behind the scenes he was married several times, with his personal life once described as "tumultuous."

"There were those stories," Connor told me. "He was nothing but delightful in working with him and we became close friends for the rest of his life. I adored Doug."

His big break came in being cast as "Trampas" in *NBC's* big budget Western series, he Virginian." He would play the character for almost a decade and received wide acclaim for his portrayal.

After "The Virginian" ended its run, he found a few films that didn't do much before finding his way into *The Land That Time Forgot* and Connor's world.

That's where we pick up with Doug McClure.

"We had to have an American star," Connor remembered. American producer and distributor Samuel Z. Arkoff and his *American International Pictures* would not come in with financing for *The Land That Time Forgot* unless there was an American male lead.

Connor took no issue with this as the script called for an American tough guy. "It was also about boxoffice and all of that." I loved how Connor put financial performance second to just making fun films with good people and all of them having a great time.

Boxoffice performance guaranteed Connor could keep doing what he was doing with the people he enjoyed, but it wasn't governing his every move. He went with things as they unfolded and adapted.

"I thought we were going to get this guy who was in American Westerns."

That guy was Stuart Whitman who was sought to play the starring role of American Bowen Tyler. While he was known for his Western films and TV roles, he was also a well known face on American TV crime shows. He was the "I've seen that guy!" Guy.

The ever popular "creative differences" along with scheduling problems took Whitman out of the running.

"Max [Rosenberg] had gone ahead and booked this guy [Whitman] and paid him. Arkoff came along and said, 'Oh no, no, no, we don't want this guy. We want another Western actor.' "

Coincidentally, the Western TV actor Richard Boone, known for his role as Paladin on the hit TV Western "Have Gun—Will Travel" would go on to headline his own dinosaur movie, *The Last Dinosaur* in an *ABC Friday Night Movie.*

It never occurred to Connor that it was Doug McClure Arkoff wanted. "I didn't know who Doug McClure was. I didn't even know the name of who Arkoff wanted, I had some other guy in mind."

Connor was told this new star was Trampas and he had never heard of Trampas but accepted that this was the guy production wanted and that was that.

This is where I am impressed with Connor's ability to put himself aside, his ego, whatever you want to call it, to understand that it truly is about the bigger picture.

He has a crew and other things to attend and the battle to fight the powers that be that write the checks is often a hill one does not wish to die on even when they think they should.

As a director, I see Kevin Connor as someone who knew exactly the kind of film he was making, how it should be handled and deftly steered through the pre-production minefields that often delay or derail motion pictures.

McClure flew to England after speaking with Connor to shoot *Land* and met the director for the first time.

"This actor arrived who Sam approved of and it turned out to be Doug McClure!"

They had lunch in London a few days after he arrived and Connor realized that this was not the guy he thought he was.

"He was one of the boys. This big, 6'4 guy. Handsome guy and I could see why they wanted him for the part. We got on very well and we moved forward."

A little over a week later McClure arrived on set at Shepperton Studios for costume fittings and script discussions. Sets were being built and director and lead hit it off.

"He was a fun-loving guy. Loved to go out on the town (not that I went with him often) and a wonderful piece of casting."

McClure loved to work and gave Connor the impression that he might not always read the script. It didn't matter, he was happy to be there and we would give everything to the role and the production.

"He wasn't from a career to be a big Hollywood star. He was doing TV and I don't think he even asked how we would pull off the dinosaurs. He wasn't interested in the mechanics of how we would do the scenes."

"I'll do whatever you want me to do, Bro," McClure told the director. He was there to do a good job and in the hands of his director and the production.

"He was so cooperative. Never problems shooting with him on the set. He was so easy."

McClure did bring with him his talent and instinct for placing a punch perfectly for the camera. Having done numerous fight scenes for TV, McClure was kind of his own fight coordinator, and his ability to throw the punches at the right angle, with on spot timing, saved a lot of retakes and time shooting those scenes.

"He knew where to be to throw the punch. Really first class awareness of the camera. Saved us a lot of time. An actor isn't always so great at these things and you have to worry about safety to ensure he doesn't knock out the other guy. That wasn't the case with Doug."

McClure made suggestions and improvements to the scenes which saved time and endeared him to Connor and the crew.

"I wasn't given any approval over hiring Doug, but I am glad it turned out that way. I miss him very much."

Some reading this may wonder how Connor could not have any idea who McClure was. There was no Internet, no *IMDb* or other resources in your hand to do a quick check. There are major British stars and celebrities today who escape my awareness and I work in this industry.

Not everything is American-centric as Americans like to believe.

"You had thing called *The Spotlight* which had all the photos of actors but they were British, not American. I had to take the word of Max and Milton that this is the guy we're going to have. Even they didn't really know his name. Arkoff insisted on that caliber of name which was perfect in this kind of movie."

The two would form a lifelong friendship that kept them in touch with each other. It also helped that McClure, coming out of a divorce, fell in love with producer John Dark's production secretary, Diane. They married and of course Diane had to be replaced.

"He had a very good sense of humor with a lot of fun tied to him. He liked to party, but he wasn't crazy." Connor attended dinners at McClure's home and he said that the cowboy image was just a persona.

"I do remember though, Doug once punched a hole right through the wall in John Dark's office. He punched right through the drywall. He wanted to go off somewhere with a few hours to spare and wanted to commandeer the production car and was denied. He got angry and in a fit, punched the hole." He quickly and profusely apologized.

John Dark framed that hole. He never repaired it. He put a frame around that broken wall section.

The crew loved Doug, as he was seen as one of the boys. He was conscious of the set and the cameras, moving lights himself to save the trouble for the crew. "He was totally at home on our sets. Never held us up. You never had to wait for him. He always knew his lines."

Only praise as a friend and actor for McClure came from Connor.

McClure succumbed to lung cancer after a long bout in 1995.

"He left us far too early," Connor lamented. "I have nothing but praise and the fondest memories of him."

Doug and Jackie McClure, Kevin Connor
and *Land* co-star Susan Penhaligon.

Kevin Connor on the frozen sub set on H Stage.

WHEN DINOSAURS RULED

I covered the options for dinosaur special effects and what technologies were available at the time. From the outset, Connor decided to go with creatures that were not men in suits or time consuming, expensive stop motion animation.

The Land That Time Forgot would use puppetry.

This is interesting because the film was a total Western film—made in Britain, by a Western studio but the choice to go with puppetry evoked the ancient art of *Bunraku* which was Japanese puppetry and storytelling. While that Eastern process involved marionettes and puppets operated by hand and long sticks, this has a nice connection to the kaiju end of things that was dominated by Japan and *Toho Studios* from the 1954 and to that time.

The special effects team had been working pre-production with production designer, Maurice Carter.

A film production designer is responsible for the overall visual concept and design of a film. Their role involves creating the film's visual style, including the sets, costumes, props, and overall look of the film's environment. They work closely with the director and other key members of the production team to bring the film's creative vision to life. Production designers collaborate with various departments to ensure that the visual elements align with the film's narrative, tone, and themes. They manage the artistic and practical aspects of set construction, decoration, and location scouting. Ultimately, the production designer's work contributes significantly to the film's aesthetic and storytelling impact.

Carter was a renowned production designer and art director in the film

industry. He was born on March 6, 1910, in Hyde, Cheshire, England, and his career spanned several decades, during which he made significant contributions to numerous films before dying in 1994.

Carter's work encompassed a wide range of genres and styles, from period dramas to fantasy and adventure films. He was known for his meticulous attention to detail and his ability to create immersive and authentic visual worlds that enhanced the storytelling on screen.

This is seen in *The Land That Time Forgot* and its sequel, *The People That Time Forgot*, with such consistency in production design details, the two films look as if they were shot back to back.

This would carry over into the interim film, *At the Earth's Core*, where even as a boy I could tell that the look of the film bore strong resemblance to *The Land That Time Forgot* and then *The People That Time Forgot*, which I saw as part of that drive-in double bill.

Carter's role as a production designer involved creating the visual concept and overall look of a film. He worked closely with directors, cinematographers, and other members of the creative team to translate the script's vision into tangible sets, props, and visual elements.

He was one of the first to use the front projection visual effects process and went on to found The British Film Designers Guild.

His work encompassed designing interior and exterior locations, as well as overseeing the construction and dressing of sets to ensure they accurately reflected the film's time period, genre, and narrative.

Carter's contributions to cinema earned him recognition and accolades in the industry. He was nominated for an Academy Award for Best Art Direction-Set Decoration for *The Great Gatsby* (1974), directed by Jack Clayton.

Carter's job for *The Land That Time Forgot* was setting the tone, and the feel and look of the world. The dinosaur effects would need to blend in with his art design so that one visual piece doesn't look like it stands out from the others.

When you look at the other dinosaur films that used real lizards, you get this kind of askew view—it just doesn't seem right. It's akin to the "Uncanny Valley" that feeling when we watch CGI and digital human figures that just don't seem right to us.

The dinosaur puppets in *Land* had to look like they inhabited this world and this is where Carter nailed it. He created the world for these creatures to live.

Imagine the Japanese production design of giant cities in the old *Godzilla* or *Ultraman* series. Think about the hand painted backdrops and skies, the plaster buildings and often that harsh studio light.

Now drop in the kaiju creature Suitmation actors and you often have monster costumes that compliment this very Eastern surrealism that is not going for reality. Growing up I grew accustomed to that surreal, often hokey look of *Tsuburaya Productions* and the kaiju destruction that came out of my TV.

Go further and take those Japanese sets—the buildings, the backdrops, the giant pools that serve as oceans, and add in the realistic kaiju digital monsters of today. Take *Jurassic Park* or *Legendary Pictures Godzilla* realism and put that into the old model sets.

It won't mesh.

I noted this clash of production and art design with 1977's *The Last Dinosaur* which was a co-production between US-based Rankin-Bass Entertainment and Tsuburaya Studios of Japan. The end result was disjointed at best.

The American team came in expecting realism, with American-style action and less reliance on surreal abstract imagery.

The studio work—the miniatures, the sets and the design of the T-rex suit for the Suitmation process proved a major disappointment for a number of the American cast involved.

When you watch the film the clash in Eastern and Western artistic styles results in a viewing experience that turned a number of American audiences off and created the sense that the film was a flop.

It was not, but its main stars found the special effects lacking and the clash of cultures diminishing their work and I think this all relayed to people watching.

This was not the case with *The Land That Time Forgot*. Carter's production design worked in close alliance with Roger Dicken and his dinosaur concepts. The entire film fused well with the live-action shots and made for a consistent motion picture experience that rarely took us out of the world Connor took us into.

"It was Maurice who found Roger Dicken who made these things and he had a whole range of other animals that he created. The whole thing about Roger Dickens was the detail in the animals. He didn't want to make just a regular old monster; he wanted a genuine Triceratops or whatever."

The puppetry allowed for director of photography Alan Hume to get close on the beasts as they could be crafted more meticulously than what usual suitmation allowed. By shooting at normal speed instead of frame by frame like stop motion animation, the camera could hold longer on the subjects, and allow the audience to experience the creatures in real time.

The animated puppetry he pioneered infused life into models that, while limited in their range compared to animation, bore the advantage of swiftness in execution. The puppets, while not endowed with the versatility of stop-motion animation, possessed a unique dynamism. They could forge through tangible undergrowth, engaging with elements like fog, mist, and water effects in a seamless symphony of the fantastical.

They also made for terrific close-ups. The camera loved them.

With hand to hand coordination, Dicken and his brigade of assistants orchestrated the movements of these monumental puppet beings before the discerning eye of the camera. These mechanical marvels, around the size of dogs, portrayed the Allosaurus and Styracosaurus, mirroring their imposing scale. The audacious endeavor didn't only manifest in the triumphant creations but extended to encompass an intricate collaboration.

He did not operate the full-sized Plesiosaur head, crafted in the plasterer's sanctum that drew life from his small-scale model. Nor did he operate the soaring Pterodactyls, and all their fiberglass grandeur, as they were animated with a crane—which we will discuss more later.

There was no characteristic frame "flicker" with puppetry as one saw with stop motion. The process had this inherent defect. Today some of Harryhausen's old work from *Jason and the Argonauts* has been digitally restored to allow a more fluid frame speed to give more realistic motion to his creations than what normal allowed at that time.

"I think Maurice Carter and his art director Bert Davey were behind getting Dicken into the fold."

Connor told me of his pleasure to have effects designer Derek Meddings on board. He integrated with Roger Dicken with the practical dinosaurs to round out this team.

Meddings was a British special effects designer and artist known for his groundbreaking work in film and television with a career that spanned several decades, during which he contributed his talents to create captivating visual effects in some of the most iconic films in history, including James Bond and Superman.

Meddings began his career in the film industry in the 1950s, working as a draughtsman and designer on various productions. He worked with matte paintings and quickly moved into other visual effects areas. He gained prominence for his work on the James Bond franchise, starting with *Thunderball* in 1965, where he created innovative underwater sequences using miniatures and practical effects. His meticulous attention to detail and dedication to achieving realism set the stage for his future accomplishments.

His career took a significant turn when he joined forces with producer Gerry Anderson on various television projects. He contributed to the creation of iconic series like "Thunderbirds" and "Captain Scarlet and the Mysterons" (1967-1968).

My weekend afternoons were made up of multiple viewings of these episodes every chance I could get. The puppets were animated marionettes, again invoking an Eastern Bunraku style that was both captivating and sometimes a little creepy.

I think "Thunderbirds" and "Captain Scarlet" (I can still hear its theme song) might some of the first examples of pop culture "Uncanny Valley." Take a look at these online and you will see what I mean.

Meddings' expertise in model work, miniature sets, and pyrotechnics was instrumental in bringing these puppet-based shows to life. His designs of futuristic vehicles, elaborate sets, and explosive sequences became a hallmark of Anderson's productions.

Cars flew off cliffs and exploded, rockets blasted off launch pads and evil villain bases blew up. This would later inspire me as an early teen to blow up my models in the back yard to get the thrill in real time.

Meddings moved into the 70s with director Richard Donner on *Superman* (1978). This would earn him a BAFTA Award. His work on the film's visual effects, including Superman's flying sequences and the destruction of Krypton, , the still fantastic crumbling of the Hoover Dam and the impressive Golden Gate Bridge miniature work showcased his ability to seamlessly integrate practical effects with new technologies. You can see his style and work in that film's opening as the lighting and miniature work reflects direct visual connections to *The Land That Time Forgot*'s cataclysmic ending.

Meddings' connection to the James Bond franchise persisted, and spanned multiple Bond films all the way up to Pierce Brosnan's films including *GoldenEye* (1995) and *Tomorrow Never Dies*" (1997). His ability to craft intricate miniature models and explosive practical effects continued to enhance the cinematic experience. He also worked on other notable films like *Aliens*, Tim Burton's *Batman* (1989), and *Judge Dredd* (1995).

Looking back it's clear that Meddings had a signature style to his miniature work. I expressed my admiration for the miniatures in *Land That Time Forgot* in talking with Connor, but the Bond films like *The Spy Who Loved Me* and *Moonraker* rushed back to me. That famous underwater *Lotus* car in *The Spy Who Loved Me* was thanks to Meddings' miniature work intercut with a full sized vehicle.

The villain's lair and supertankers that swallowed submarines was impressive even then, utilizing real sunlight and camera techniques that blew me away on the big screen.

Meddings was able to show producers like the Salkinds or Albert Broccoli that you didn't need expensive, massive full-sized sets. He was able to give the depth and scope of massive villain lairs and settings with cheaper alternatives that didn't look cheap.

Jonah Ray said a line in the *Mystery Science Theater* episode on *The Land That Time Forgot*: "This is what every *Star Wars* movie looks like before the CGI."

While it was meant as a snarky dig at a shot of the WW I sub rising from the ocean, I took it as a compliment. All these decades later and that miniature work still holds up.

I will go through this in a scene examination of the film that applies all of this information to the actual execution of these effects later in this book.

I stand by it. That snark was a dig at a man nominated for an Oscar for his effects on *Moonraker*, a Special Achievement Award for *Superman* and several other *BAFTA* nominations.

Meddings set up his own effects company at Shepperton Studios called *The Magic Camera Company* and was asked to work on *Batman* because Tim Burton was a fan of his work on "Thunderbirds."

In your face, *MST3K*.

All of these "parts" created a great sum with Connor's effects team. *The Land That Time Forgot* was about more than puppet dinosaurs. Without all of the elements listed above, the film would have been a cheap knockoff film meant for late night TV programming graveyards.

Yet, this was a film that held me spellbound as a boy and impressed me far greater than the more expensive *King Kong* remake.

How is this possible?

Part of the answer lies in Connor's team building and unified visions. This is something the 1976 *Kong* lacked. From an effects and production design point of view, *King Kong* looked like a patchwork of artists who worked their own departments but there was little effort made in a unified vision.

Understanding what visual effects are and the direction they are headed is key.

Another factor was when John Dark, producer for *The Land That Time Forgot*, sought an alternative to conventional animation. A distinct vision led him to an artist who would chart a new course for special effects. In a creative twist, this individual embarked on devising the activated puppet technique that would grace the film.

Dicken would go on to be nominated for the 1971 feature *When Dinosaurs Ruled the Earth* (Which Spielberg gave a nice nod to at the end of *Jurassic Park* when the banner falls from the ceiling around the roaring T-rex). He would also create and do the puppetry for 1979's *Alien* with its infant Xenomorph and its progenitor Facehugger.

He often expressed his love of monsters and creating them. Born in Portsmouth, Hampshire in England, he grew up on horror and adventure films. Dicken embarked on his creative journey armed not with formal artistic education, but with the fragments of knowledge he gleaned from school.

The essence of creativity had always coursed through his veins, a fact affirmed by an old clairvoyant who perceived a special 'gift' within him since birth. This innate drive became the force propelling his endeavors onto both the silver screen and various artistic realms.

During the early 1960s, he found solace in the rented space above a worn garage, an intimate haven where he breathed life into masks, curious artifacts, and dared to explore the uncharted territory of 8mm dinosaur animation. A whimsical group of companions from Portsmouth joined hands, giving birth to *The Doctor Lugani Horror Show*.

This comedic-horror spectacle showcased his dexterity in crafting props and his metamorphic stage presence as 'Lugani,' the enigmatic Master of 'Cemeteries.' These performances unfurled in cozy venues, charming audiences with an array of ethereal apparitions — from The Hunchback to Dracula and The Wolfman. A crescendo of theatrical mastery was achieved as he swiftly transformed into the formidable Frankenstein's Monster, leaving a girl from the audience in awe at the show's climax.

The allure of Ray Harryhausen's mesmerizing animated monster epics soon captivated his heart. A fortuitous encounter with the maestro himself during the production of *Mysterious Island* resulted in an invitation to Shepperton Studios. There, amidst the filmic enchantment, he witnessed the intricate constructs of model air balloons and puppet squids from the Nemo sequences. Ray's warmth and the magic of the studio back lots kindled a fervor that beckoned him to the realm of filmmaking.

Upon relocating to London, he found his foothold within the hallowed halls of the *BBC*. Here, his touch graced the studios as he ventured deeper into the art of stagecraft. Yet, a deeper passion urged him forth. The invitation to participate in Kubrick's monumental *2001* presented a crossroads: forsaking the comforts of a nine-to-five existence, he embarked on a freelance odyssey. Amid the constellation of artistic souls, he lent his hand to crafting miniature lunar landscapes, contributing to the grandeur of the production.

"Guys like Dicken and the others worked on major feature films. Major ones," Connor reminded me. I was lucky to access or be presented with these creative people and their experience in how they made films cleverly instead of just throwing money at it."

Charles Staffell was the "go to guy" for back and front projection. As noted, while neither photographic technology was new, it was the quality of the effects plate for the eventual print that mattered most.

His meticulous attention to detail and commitment to achieving realism set him apart as a master of his craft. As stated earlier his career went on to encompass films like *Superman* and *Superman II* and Cameron's *Aliens*.

Staffell's collaboration with filmmakers of note elevated his profile within the industry. His innovative contributions to films like *The Land That Time Forgot* demonstrated his ability to seamlessly integrate practical effects with live-action sequences, bringing fantastical worlds to life on the silver screen.

This is why the assembly of such a prominent crew benefited Connor's vision. All of these components worked outside of their respective departments to focus on the bigger picture of a cohesive visual aspect of the film.

The world of science fiction and fantasy cinema became a canvas for Staffell's creative expression. His work on films such as *The People That Time Forgot*" further showcased his skill in animating creatures and monsters, effectively immersing audiences in captivating narratives.

Rounding out this effects and Medding's team was Ian Wingrove who is uncredited in *The Land That Time Forgot*. He served overall as an assistant to Derek Meddings who was discussed earlier.

Meddings, an accomplished effects artist, carved a distinguished niche for himself in the realm of visual effects with his remarkable talent, innovation, and dedication. His journey in the world of filmmaking is marked by a series of influential collaborations and groundbreaking contributions that have left an indelible mark on the industry.

His creative vision and technical prowess earned him the respect and admiration of colleagues and peers. Medding's ability to collaborate with directors and producers to realize their visions further solidified his reputation as a valued member of the filmmaking community.

Throughout his career, he left an indelible impact on the visual effects landscape with Connor again reminding me how lucky he was to have this team of gifted artists on his films.

"It was a different time," Connor confirmed. "It really was."

Mubi.com

Courtesy Modelshipsinthecinema.com

Modelshipsinthecinema.com

MGM Studios

Top Left: Derek Meddings, miniature, model builder, and effects artist Bottom Left: Roger Dicken, dinosaur effects artists, puppeteer. Ian Wingrove, model designer.

MGM Studios

The famed Shepperton Studio H pool/tank where the sub and open ocean scenes were filmed.

MGM Studios

IT TAKES A VILLAGE

I wanted to know how Connor dealt with the top-heavy behind camera talent he was given and amassed. At this point, I got the impression that Connor wasn't a "hands off" director, but rather worked the hat trick of being the opposite but also allowing his crew—these experts, to do their jobs without his interference.

Connor is a director that knows the value of someone's expertise and makes no moves to counter that with ego or control. He is not a task master, but as the interview progressed I got to understand a film director who knew that the bigger picture was in fact—the big picture.

"It's about knowing what sells as well, too." He recalled a moment where *American International* wanted more "dinosaur action." Connor could have easily thrown down a line and refused. His vision for the film was a vision for financial and commercial success, so if the distributor wanted more dinosaurs he would oblige.

"I believe we shot this extra scene with a dinosaur protecting its eggs or something along that line," he recalled. It gave the opportunity to re-create the now iconic scene from a dozen children's dinosaur books depicting the T-Rex and Triceratops battle that seems to come to everyone's mind when they think of dinosaurs.

"We storyboarded everything," Connor told me. "We did that with Maurice Carter. I sat down and we spent lots of time storyboarding."

He invoked the first dinosaur attack on the hapless German atop the submarine upon arriving in Caprona. "Doug had to fight with the head of something. He's fighting this creature that was trying to get into the tower of the sub. We built this giant rubber mechanical head, beautifully detailed and the rubber texture was splendid.

Four or five guys would hold and wheel it around and drop it on Doug, "WHACK!" and whatever. So we built bits and pieces of big monsters for particular shots."

Connor's editing background gave him the ability to know what shots he wanted, allowing more efficiency in the planning process. He knew what he wanted in close up or what would be done with inserts.

This created shorthand between Connor as a director and the artists around him who were tasked to realizing his vision. It sounded completely free-flowing and easy instead of Connor demanding, dictating and controlling.

These days it would be said that Kevin Connor knew how to stay in his lane. He gave free hands to the people around him and trusted them in their knowledge of their crafts and skills.

"We did go through everything with them and broke it all down. Maurice worked them up as boards and that's how each little bit was worked out beforehand.

You need to storyboard things because some it will be part second unit as well and all of that needs to be accounted for. You have to make sure they get the right shots."

Ways had to be found to keep the budget in line. This is tough with a big dinosaur action film. The trick was relying on not just the puppeteers of the creatures but also your art designers, visual effects artists as well to get in close on these creatures without giving it all away.

Lighting, set design, cinematography, plate construction…it was a village of artists that came together to get these shots. "The detail in these dinosaur puppets allowed us to get in really close.

By the time you got the smoke around it or whatever it was—trees, bamboo—everyone allowed this to work so well."

I asked about the twin dinosaur effect shot—the meat eating Allosaurs where McClure and crew confronted them and shot them dead. I asked if Connor was hands on in directing these scenes or did he leave that to a second unit to get this stuff while Connor focused more on the big action set pieces and his actors.

"There really wasn't a second unit," he told me. "I directed all the inserts and model work. We had two weeks to do that before we started principal photography. I was there for all of it. The final scene where we blow everything up...I was there for all of that."

Connor stopped here to tell me a special effects story that didn't just impress me, but rather reinforced everything I was doing since I was a kid. It gave me joy to know that this man and his team could be so damned resourceful.

In the opening of *Land* there is a scene where the WW I German U-boat sinks a passenger liner—the very one that will lead to McClure and his merry troupe to take over said sub.

"In the periscope you see this tramp steamer, passenger ship or whatever on the skyline. It cost like maybe 25 dollars to make that shot."

I was astounded. Under a hundred bucks to shoot a major scene like that? How?

"We were already filming in the tank," Connor went on. "Derek Meddings, who would go on to be a major effects guy—found a model of a ship in the hallways of Shepperton Studios. It was just on show in a glass case. It happened to be one of the transport ships, you know?

Well Derek took off the glass case and took a picture of it. You know—a black and white photo of this model ship. He developed it, blew up the photo, stuck it way at the end of the tank, at horizon line of the water, and put a little funnel up the back."

Meddings pasted that ship photo to some hard board, then pumped smoke through the funnel he affixed to the back of the two dimensional photo of the ship and create the illusion of this being a three dimensional model in the distance.

When you watch the scene, the visual team improves on Meddings' brilliant cost-saving miniature work by adding the periscope overlay which obfuscates any inherent flaws and makes the illusion complete.

I was astounded in hearing this because all these decades I thought it was a functioning real model ship and all it was--a photo glued to hard board. I stole this right away.

I produced a terrific supernatural thriller presently in post at the time of this writing. The scene called for an underwater view of a rowboat on the surface. It is a character point of view shot as they sink to the bottom of a lake.

We did not have the time or budget at that time to set up a scene for shooting underwater and getting the real boat. I took what Connor told me and borrowed Derek Meddings' idea. I cut out a piece of cardboard, maybe four inches in length, encased it in black think plastic and floated it in a 20 gallon aquarium.

I lit it up right, applied a transparent garbage bag overtop the tank and colored the water with milk and used Efferdent tablets to give some color and bubbles. I placed the two dimensional black cardboard shape on the surface and shot from the bottom up through tank and boom…Derek Meddings and his miniature strategy worked all these years later.

"It wasn't a stop motion shot or large model shot. He just took a picture and we shot it through the periscope and what do you

Modelshipsinthecinema.com

The photographs of ships used in place of models in the first act of *Land That Time Forgot.*

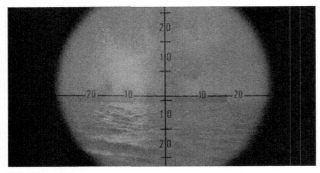

Modelshipsinthecinema.com

This was genius in its simplicity and innovation.

MGM Studios

The SOS scene where real Morse Code was used because art designer Bert Davey served in WW II and knew how to signal.

know…25 dollars. You always have to be of the mind to save a dollar wherever possible and I was all for it. Quite creative, I must say."

"We did hand over the mechanical dinosaur head that attacked them on the sub to a second unit. It always took a little while to get things credible. We got it to where you believed it. So we couldn't stop main photography for something like that and spend two days to play around."

Director of Photography Alan Hume led this crew of artists for those weeks of pre-production where the miniature shots were done. "I never told Alan his job. I knew how things should look and conveyed that to him but that was his job to get it that way."

These artistic "villagers" all met in those early two weeks where questions would be asked of all the departments. Costume designers were asked by the photography folks what colors would be used for the actors outfits, lighting was asked questions, the miniatures crew asked the same—a lot of back and forth departmental communication which allowed for an efficient and overall drama-free shoot.

"You coordinate everything and that's all done in pre-production. That's where a lot of the ground is laid and where the money is saved."

It was this kind of coordination that impressed me with the unified visual consistency of the film. Everything seemed to dovetail together. While each artists wants to leave their mark, if one part becomes heavier, then it creates imbalance in visual and artistic style. As mentioned, this was a major issue for 1977's *The Last Dinosaur*.

Matte paintings are essential to a film like this. While Meddings had worked with matte in his career, the matte paintings for *Land* were designed by Cliff Culley.

Culley was behind the scenes at Rank's Pinewood Studios, and played an instrumental role in numerous productions spanning a variety of genres. His entry in the world of special effects was in 1946 when he joined Pinewood's special effects department under the leadership of Bill Warrington. During this period, the renowned Les Bowie headed the matte painting department until his departure in 1949, subsequently passing the torch to the legendary Albert Whitlock, who held this position from 1949 to 1953.

Culley's career trajectory took an exciting turn when he collaborated with industry giants like Peter Ellenshaw and Whitlock, contributing his expertise to Disney's *Sword and the Rose* in 1953. It was here that he honed his skills as a matte painting specialist, a role that would define much of his career. Over the years, Culley participated in a multitude of film projects, ultimately ascending to the prestigious position of head of Pinewood's matte painting department in the mid to late 1960s.

His talents extended beyond matte painting, as Culley was responsible for crafting numerous optical gags that added a touch of magic to various films. Notably, he orchestrated the memorable reflection of a thug in the eye of a beautiful girl in the opening scene of *Goldfinger*.

However, it is his supervisory role in matte art that truly solidified Culley's legacy. His work can be found in the James Bond classics *You Only Live Twice* and *On Her Majesty's Secret Service,* as well as the whimsical *Chitty Chitty Bang Bang.* The latter stands as one of his primary screen credits in a supervisory capacity, alongside *One of Our Dinosaurs is Missing, Spaceman in King Arthur's Court* for Disney, and *Hellraiser II.*

Culley came on board to do the matte work for Connor in both *Land That Time Forgot* and *People.*

He took on new talent to give them a chance and collaborated on Connors *Warlords of Atlantis* and other projects like 1981's *Clash of the Titans.*

Culley contributed animated matte work that can be seen on the arrival at Caprona. The huge Diplodocus on the mountain is Culley's work along with the animated birds over the jungle skyline.

"Cliff did a lot of work on my next two films, and he would steal the look of Frank Frazetta for the feel of my films. A little influence there," Connor chuckled.

Connor lamented that today everything is done by video conferencing where he believed the best way to get things done was getting people into a room together. Nothing substitutes for face to face interaction—something a daily visit to social media can support.

Connor emphasized that the times back then were harder and people simply wanted to work. This amazing pool of talent came together for this dinosaur action film when some may wonder... why?

It was a different time. It wasn't about ego. It was about working.

That different time translates into what it is like today where Connor feels directors have to be more cutthroat than when he was doing his earlier films.

"There are so many producers and bean counters. This executive producer, this associate producer, this title, that title...directors need to fight harder to keep their visions because of so much studio interference."

This is where I feel somber and maudlin in talking with Connor. It was a different time, truly an era that time has forgotten...when people came together to do their best to just make something good.

The word "Content" is anathema to creativity and art. Am I calling *The Land That Time Forgot* art? Yeah, maybe I am because despite it being relegated to *Mystery Science Theater* territory, I think these last chapters laid out the case that some pretty damned talented artists came together in the spirit of making something good.

That's not like the cynical, over-priced, expensive content we get today. Go back and look at what was playing in movie theaters in 1974-1975 and then compare it to what is out there today.

You will be hard-pressed to find a sequel in that early 70s lineup or not a remake to be found. "Sequel" and "remake" were still low-brow, dirty words to the industry back then. "Franchise" was relegated to fast food.

"Everybody worked to try and make a good film. No one works to make a bad film."

Maybe not back then, but that's not the case now.

There is a difference between "So bad it's good" and just plain "bad."

"You don't get the intimacy watching a film like you used to. Nowadays there are 600 people in an auditorium. It's not the same atmosphere. You don't get the kick out of being in that dark room these days and feel like you're watching magic anymore."

Connor conceded he was glad he was not starting out today in this industry.

How exactly did *Amicus* and *American International* see *The Land That Time Forgot* with all of these people behind it? Was this a serious adult-action film or for the kids?

"It was more of a Saturday morning film, you know? A film where mom and dad could take the kids and enjoy it. When we had the premiere for *Land*, they didn't invite the press. They invited kids and packed the theater with these kids.

The kids took me back to my childhood theatrical viewings. Kids shouting, booing the Germans, cheering the good guys, cat-calling in the love scenes."

That's exactly how I went into the film as a boy. My father loved big monster movies and he wanted to be as entertained as I was. For me and I think for him, *The Land That Time Forgot* delivered.

"They never wanted to up the budget to make it a bigger film," Connor said. "There was also some political stuff going on behind the scenes at that time between John Dark, Max and Milton. They were suing each other. Milton hated John Dark, for whatever reasons, but I always felt John knew his business in making films and gave us free range to do things."

It all showed as I reminded Connor again, for the third or fourth time that his film delivered far more thrills and fun than the incredibly expensive *King Kong* remake that would debut just a little under two year later.

"I ate it up," I told him.

Connor laughed and said, "We had flying dinosaurs, walking dinosaurs, swimming dinosaurs…"

"It was jam packed," I agreed.

Once again…just one big, dopey rubber snake in *King Kong*.

My memory was corrected on the film's performance. For me, I felt it was a huge film. Kids at school saw it, we all talked about it and it played at one of the first modern "Twin Theaters" in our area, not some hole-in-the-wall small town house. I saw *Earthquake* at this Twin and eventually *Jaws 2* and *Close Encounters*.

"No," Connor sighed. "It didn't do all that well. Not like you are thinking. "I think it did okay, but it didn't make *Amicus* a fortune. I mean it allowed us to make two more. We did a sequel and then *At the Earth's Core* so there had to be something there."

Connor might be a bit too modest. In terms of box office performance, *The Land That Time Forgot* fared well commercially. It performed solidly at the box office and was successful enough to spawn *The People That Time Forgot*. It was the 14th highest grossing film in Britain that year.

I commented on the unsung village artist, often forgotten...the artist who did the posterwork for *The Land That Time Forgot*. "That poster was phenomenal," I exclaimed.

"It was. It truly was," Connor agreed.

That artist was Tom Chantrell. While he did a number of posters for big box-office hits, Chantrell's most famous artwork is arguably the original poster for 1977's *Star Wars* with Luke standing over Leia, thrusting the lightsaber above his head.

The poster for *The Land That Time Forgot* is spectacular even today. Hand-drawn...no Photoshop or AI art. Real art...not content. I challenge you to not get excited for dinosaur action when looking at the poster for *The Land That Time Forgot*.

This collection of artists came together and because of Connor's laid back, pleasant and respectful demeanor as a director, were allowed to deliver top stuff and to be creative in the making of a film that was not "content."

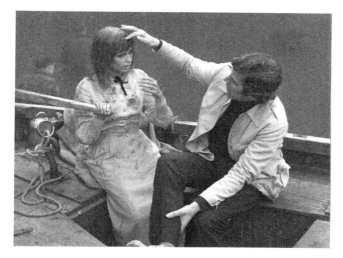

Kevin Connor works with star, Susan Penhaligon on the set of *The Land That Time Forgot* in the giant Studio H pool and tank.

Below, special effects artist, George Gibbs who worked on *Land* but also contributed to 1984's *Indiana Jones and the Temple of Doom.*

ukpetercushing
appreciationsociety

Special Effects Chief GEORGE GIBBS puts the finishing tweak on magic carpet and guards on set of 'ARABIAN ADVENTURE'

Mubi.com
Samuel Z. Arkoff

Mubi.com
Max Rosenberg

Mubi.com
Charles Staffell

Mubi.com
Milton Subotsky

Mubi.com
Julie Harris

Mubi.com
John Dark

Alan Hume

Derek Meddings

Douglas Gamely

Roger Dicken

Michael Moorcock

THE THICK OF IT...

"I loved the script," Connor said. It was already written by the time he came to the project. "I thought it was a great Saturday morning movie type of film. I was really thrilled to be offered it. It wasn't a horror film, it was still *Amicus* and I knew it would be relatively low budget. It was a feature film, a complete story and an adventure film."

The script was written by Michael Moorcock and James Cawthorn. "I never met them, unfortunately. Moorcock did a lot of good stuff in science fiction—really interesting stories."

Milton Subotsky took his turn at rewriting the script. "Whether that was the one the two gentlemen did or the one that Milton futzed around with—I do not know if what I got was the original script before Milton took his turn."

"If anything was deleted from the script it was to save a few pounds which would have been in conjunction with the producers and the production designer."

Connor went along with the consulting because he was also learning as he went being *Land* was his only his second directing assignment. "I listened and took advice, watching them do their thing to make sure costs didn't overlap, that kind of thing."

Talking with Connor brought to mind the cost-saving practices on Paramount's *Star Trek II: The Wrath of Khan*. The original 1979 *Star Trek the Motion Picture* was infamously expensive to make and did only okay boxoffice when it all shook out.

Excitement for a sequel was guarded and cautious at best, and the second time around the budget would be reigned in and more attention would be on costs. This was seen in redressing the bridge of *The Enterprise* to double for the bridge of the enemy ship, *Reliant* commandeered by Khan. New uniforms would be introduced but they would stay with the cast for several more films to the point where Shatner joked they were falling apart long after *Wrath of Khan*.

"Production would do something similar. We would use a set, then drag it out of storage, repaint it, touch it up, make a few changes and off we would go."

I talked of re-using back lot sets as they did for *Back to the Future, Gremlins* and *Fright Night*...they are all the same "town" just dressed differently. "It's common sense," Connor agreed. "That's what I loved about it—making use of things already at your disposal. Makes sense. It's easier with 200 million to make a film to throw at a set because a director can't make up their mind. On our level, you have to commit yourself sometimes to a three wall set or even a two wall set!"

Connor stood by designing shots in advance to save money and how important it was to have the right production designers and art directors to save a buck without compromising on quality.

Most of the film would be shot at Shepperton Studios. I asked about the opening credits and the end scene depicting very different topography than the tropical settings in the main body of the film.

"The opening and end scenes were shot on the Isle of Skye in Scotland. It was all shot prior to the main unit of the film. I went up there with my helicopter cameraman, Peter Allwork. He would go on to film the incredible aerial sequences for *Out of* Africa.

It was just myself, the location manager, an assistant or second assistant director. We flew way up into the sky, landed in the snow capped mountains and had two extras to play Doug and Susan. We had the costumes already made."

These were long shots so faces would not be seen. Peter would hang on the outside of the helicopter to get the shots. "Beautiful work," Connor exclaimed. When you watch the film and see those two actors trudging through the snow, they are not the stars and they were filmed by only several people to get the shot.

This would be the same location for the opening of Ridley Scott's *Alien* prequel, *Prometheus*, decades later.

"For the opening shots, we got a local guy from a pub; he might've been in charge of a light house or something like that. He had his uniform and was a local." Connor went on to compliment the residents on the Isle of Skye as real characters and genuine.

The opening shows this salty older seaman retrieving the yellow canister McClure will toss off a cliff at the end of the film. "We shot that one of the rocky beaches. The title sequences of the canister floating were done in Skye Harbor, with rough waves to make it look like it was traveling and all of that."

Connor directed all of this, not leaving this to a second unit. "I love directing everything. Every inch of film…with a film like this I wanted to be there for every bloody frame. It was my second film and I wanted to be there for all of it."

"My assistant director threw that yellow canister off the side of the cliff. I directed him with a walkie talkie to throw it from a certain distance so we wouldn't get his arm in frame. Those kinds of shots can take forever."

I have found that second unit "small stuff" can sometimes be more challenging than the big main stuff. In this case there were only two yellow canisters and they were being chucked into a real ocean, with real, turbulent currents that would crash up against the rocks.

If the camera is too far, you can't make out what is happening. Too close and you might not be able to follow the target. Then you have the overall issue of the actual ocean and it doing whatever the hell it wants to do with those props. Lose both your canisters, it means another trip back up there and that means adding more money to the budget. Salaries, equipment, film stock and helicopter fuel all figure in. It could be thousands of dollars to get a simple; ten second shot of a metal can thrown from a cliff.

The actual jungle scenes for the interior of Caprona were shot in what Connor called a "Sand Pit" about a mile or so from Shepperton Studios.

"It was an old sand pit in a nearby town and they had this vast area of overgrown, weird formations of old sand covered in weird brambles and in the middle of nowhere. It was like a 15 minute drive from the studio but we could do explosions and blow things up with no issues."

A big chunk of the film was also shot in the back lot of Shepperton Studios which had a real river running through it. "It wasn't that big, but big enough to row a boat. We got our scenes with them exploring in the weeds and stuff floating on the river was there at the studio itself. It had exotic trees we picked up from local nurseries and there you go—we created Caprona!"

The scene where the flying reptile grabs Ahm, the Gahlu caveman trying to save Doug McClure was shot in this sandpit area as well. "All the scenes with the tribes and their locations were all in this back lot area and sand pit."

Three total locations for *The Land That Time Forgot.*

"You would have never known it was so simple. You put a little smoke out there and transform everything. It cost nothing for us to shoot at that sand pit and the locals there loved that we wanted to blow things up." Connor chuckled at that memory.

It's important to note that Connor, Carter and other crew chiefs did these location scouts and visits off the clock, without being paid. They went above and beyond to find the right places and work together as a team for the good of the picture.

There was a great story about Connor's relationship with director of photography, Alan Hume with a particular shot of the introduction of the tribal men in the high grasses of the sand pit.

"It was magic hour," Connor recalled. Magic hour is late afternoon, usually after four when the sun gets a beautiful golden glow to it that lasts in a short window to just before dusk. It's that time cameramen love shooting because it adds such production value and sheen to a shot.

"Hume thought it was too dark," Connor told me. "I thought it all looked great and I told Alan, we should shoot this, look how good it looks."

This is where one would think director and cinematographer would clash, maybe waste that time within that window arguing and debating. Instead Hume agreed to shoot it but marked on the clapboard: "Shot under protest."

That was an English gentleman's way of noting his authority without compromising the production. It's a great small story. "He didn't have all the light he wanted but it made the final film. There was no animosity or anything like that. You had a friendship and there was no "You will shoot that" kind of thing."

There is a popular misconception that at the time this film went into production, and even now, that Edgar Rice Burroughs's books are in the public domain. This was not true for *The Land That Time Forgot* and it is not true now.

"I don't know what the cost was to license *Land*. *Amicus* bought the rights all three films of his. We also wanted to license the *John Carter* books but we couldn't work that out with cost. The money was just too much because you were paying for the Burroughs name."

Disney would go on to make *John Carter of Mars* which would become a massive boxoffice bomb. Connor attributes the film's infamous failure to it not being fun and moved too far away from the spirit of being a fun Saturday matinee kind of film.

"It was a spectacular but they blew it," Connor agreed.

Amicus turned away from the Edgar Rice Burroughs Foundation after that. It was one of the reasons why Connor would go on to make *Warlords of Atlantis*. Why spend huge sums of money licensing those when he and his team could write their own adventure, fun Saturday matinee type movies?

That's just what they did with *Warlords*.

With effects work in production before main shooting started, and opening titles and the ending scene shot, Connor was ready to move into the thick of it all with his main cast, a sub, an island and dinosaurs.

Novelist, Edgar Rice Burroughs

MGM Studios

MOVING INTO THE FILM

There is a problem with filmmaking today. There are many problems, but this one has grown over the years and has, in a way, metastasized.

The advent of cable TV, the VCR, DVD and then The Internet gave us the need to fill content. Aside from "deleted scenes" or "director's cuts," in my opinion, nothing has done more damage to filmmaking than "Bonus Features" also known as "Behind the Scenes" (BTS).

Hear me out.

Once "magic" became the thing of entertainment, and by that I mean, it moved from the religious, supernatural realms of population control with science and intellectual enlightenment exposing the con gimmicks that those kinds of things entailed—a certain amount of awe left the craft.

From carnival performances all the way through Vegas acts and David Copperfield making the Statue of Liberty disappear—audiences know they are being duped. They know the giant Lady Liberty didn't vanish from its massive base.

Throw in people like Houdini and James "The Amazing" Randi who openly exposed charlatans and magic con men, a bit of the fun left the whole experience.

In the 90s, TV shows aired "Magic's Greatest Tricks Revealed/ Exposed" specials that took even more luster away from that kind of entertainment.

As media expanded, so did our knowledge and at times it seemed the industry reliant upon magicians and illusionists was simultaneously happy to deconstruct them.

Revealing "How It's Done" was almost as entertaining as the actual performances of magic and deception. It was like major media party-pooping all over its own product.

I remember *HBO* airing "Behind The Scenes" type mini pieces between feature films as part of its programming. They did a few of these on the making of major films like *Raiders of the Lost Ark* and even the unfortunate *Jaws 3-D*.

While it was kind of cool to see how "they did it" it was also a bit like getting too good of a look behind the curtain. Some of the magic went away because now you knew exactly how it was done.

As a future filmmaker, these kind of special bits were invaluable for learning the craft. I will give it that, but when this kind of thing started becoming routine, with network TV aping the process and airing their own "making of" specials, the average movie going audience started to become an audience of know-it-alls.

You would hear people going in or out of the theater explaining how certain things were done, how effects were made and stunts were performed. They had to let everyone know they knew.

They're mojo killers. Killers of joy.

Bruce the shark was scarier when we didn't know that he broke down most of the time, that his skin often suffered from barnacles and sun-bleaching or his rubber teeth fell out. When the blue screen process of John Dykstra's work on *Star Wars* became common knowledge, the visual impact watching the films again was somewhat diminished.

I don't want to know how the magician cuts the lady in half. I want to be entertained. I don't want to know how Copperfield did his Statue of Liberty trick. I want to be amazed.

One of the last times I can remember being jaw-dropping amazed in a big screen movie was *Jurassic Park*. When that T-Rex broke out of its paddock, I turned to the girl I was with and said, "Where did they get one?" Not "How did they do it."

With CGI and green screening and all of us having access to this technology, the magic to films is at the least diminished if not gone. There was a time audiences asked "How'd they do that?!"

Now we know. Computers.

There is a trade off for knowledge. When we were little kids, we were dazzled by cartoons and even the Easter Bunny and Santa myths. The Tooth Fairy held a particular magical spot for me because she was buying body parts. Being the horror kid, what else would she want to buy one day?

Then you get older. You find out none of these things are real. You find out your toys are not made by magical elves in an arctic factory but rather in Japan and China. You put together the pieces and the wonder fades.

That's the way it goes.

Something else comes with the revealing of movie magic. It becomes cancerous to our spirit. It's the disease of cynicism.

Cynicism is anathema to entertainment. The hard work I just outlined in my work with Kevin Connor becomes relegated to the stuff of farce with *Mystery Science Theater*.

The movie magic of turning sand lots into prehistoric jungles, of making puppets thrill young audiences or cardboard photos into transport steamers becomes nothing to audiences.

We've become a spectator society of critics. We think we know everything and when it comes to films, the critics always think they can do it better. They certainly know better.

Effects are now "dated" and somehow the sleek, cold animation of CGI and green screen is preferable to matte paintings and hand crafted creatures or sets.

The knowledge turns to cynical contempt and dismissing the work of so many that gave it their all to make something to entertain. Many of these bolder films are kicked into sarcastic, snarky shows that poke fun, even good-naturedly, but the one thing that can't be denied is that many have no clue as to the passion and hard work that went into crafting the thing they dismiss.

We see this now with retrospectives on the original *Spider-Man* whose CGI is often blasted for making the film too cartoonish. Yet John Caprenter's 1982 masterpiece, *The Thing* still holds its shock and awe reputation because the practical effects to this day are better than anything computers can offer.

Kevin Connor exemplifies the fusing of art with commercial awareness. He knew how to get the job done, but he knew, above all, it was about entertainment. This is seen through all of his work.

The work behind the scenes all came together to give us a film that worked with its budget, not against it or hampered by it.

From the dinosaurs to the island of Caprona or even the WW I sub set--a lot of attention to detail went into everything.

The ocean in *The Land That Time Forgot* was a giant pool, maybe four feet deep. "It was a massive stage, and you would flood it. It was about four feet deep, coming up just above your waist. It was massive."

The sub set sat in this giant pool stage. The lagoon where the dinosaur attacks after arriving to Caprona was this water tank.

"We use it for things like the boat being torpedoed, the exterior sub set and the fights on it and so on."

The stage was called "H-Stage" and was a contained stage with no exposure to natural lighting. When you watch the scene just after the steamer's sinking, McClure and his fellow survivors are rowing through this dense fog to regroup. The lighting is stellar, looking like real, diffused sunlight. The fog was smoke fanned by people off screen and stayed so still and thick, I had to ask, "How'd you do it?"

"No, Alan got the lighting perfect along with the smoke. The rowboats go up to the full sized submarine and quietly jump on board off you go…the fight starts."

The submarine exterior and interiors were all built for the film. "The wider shots we used a 20-foot model for U-33."

The interiors were done on another stage. "It would've been nice to have the set on rollers to make it shift so we had to do it with the camera to save some money to show the movements and lurches."

The best part is production designer Maurice Carter had a German friend who had commanded a real-life U-boat. "He was a U-boat captain but I don't think during the war. Anyway, he flew over from Germany, at his own expense, to inspect our U-boat set for authenticity and detail. He gave his two bits worth for us."

The former U-boat captain gave his thumbs up to the detail and workmanship to replicate the period vehicle. "He said this is so close, you guys have done a great job."

The interiors were in this separate stage but the exteriors were in the "wet tank" on H-Stage.

All of this workmanship into this low budget dinosaur film speaks volumes. I had to keep on the U-boat theme and asked Connor about its captain, Admiral Von Schoenvorts played by actor John McEnery.

"John and Doug got along fine but we did have a problem at the end of it all. The distributor, Sam Arkoff didn't like McEnery's voice. He felt it was too feminine and we had to change it. It was "re-voiced" by another actor more to Arkoff's liking. They wanted a more guttural German voice, I guess."

McEnery was a classical theatrical actor who did a great job according to Connor. His voice was replaced by actor Anton Diffring known for his work in voicing evil Nazi bad guys.

Susan Penhaligon who plays McClure's eventual love interest, Lisa, also came from live, classical theater. It was her first film and she found it all a bit overwhelming at first.

"She was great and a good actress. I loved working with her."

McEnery took the news of his voice change with grace. "I was too embarrassed at the time to tell him," Connor said. The news delivered by the producers. "Why didn't you just bring him in and see if we could get a stronger voice out him?" Connor asked. "They had the stages and equipment, why didn't they just do that?"

It was a rhetorical question and Arkoff got his way with McEnery's voice dubbed over. This would also happen with actress Linda Hamilton in 1967's *King Kong Escapes*. Someone didn't like the actress's voice but in her case she didn't know it was changed until she saw the final film and she wasn't too happy about it.

Getting my fill of "How'd you do that?" with sets and design, I had to ask about the wardrobe for *The Land That Time Forgot*.

Keeping in mind this is a low budget film you would think the outfits would reflect this. Quite the opposite with a wardrobe designer that put the actors into not just authentic looking era clothing, but also clothing that LOOKED worn, dirty and real. This was extra attention not usually seen in lower budgeted films like this.

"Don't forget the English made our share of war films in our day," Connor reminded me. "Studios kept all of their costumes. You had access to almost every type of costume and era you could think of. It was this vast repository of wardrobe. Remember, the economy was bad and everybody wanted to work and so these places didn't charge a lot just to get the work. These costumes, as a result, were available."

The costumes were rented, and then tailored to their respective actors. John Hilling is credited as head of costumes and wardrobe but Connor recalled Julie Harris who is conspicuously missing from the film's official credits, as being the one who gave him such terrific wardrobe results. "Julie went on to work on the Bond films and I was so lucky to work with her. Her credits were nothing short of staggering. This was the caliber of people I got."

Diana Julie Harris won an Academy Award and a *BAFTA* Award. Like Connor, she went on to work for the Rank Organization, until that studio wound down its business in the 1950s.

Over the next 30 years, she worked with actors such as Jayne Mansfield, Joan Crawford, Bette Davis, Lauren Bacall and Alan Ladd and directors Alfred Hitchcock, Joseph Losey, Billy Wilder and John Schlesinger.

She made a "mink bikini" (actually made out of rabbit fur) for Diana Dors. She worked steadily on feature films throughout the next three decades, hitting her stride in the 1960s, before shifting her attention to television movies until her retirement in 1991.

Harris won the Oscar for Best Costume Design for *Darling* in 1965, and the *BAFTA* Award for Best Costume Design for *The Wrong Box* in 1967.

She also worked on the *Beatles'* first two live action feature films, *A Hard Day's Night* (1964), and *Help!* (1965), quipping that "I must be one of the few people who can claim they have seen John, Paul, George and Ringo naked."

She also worked on the James Bond film *Live and Let Die* (1973) with Roger Moore, and the spoof *Casino Royale* (1967) with David Niven.

Harris also designed costumes for the *Carry On* film *Carry On Cleo* (1964), a sword and sandal spoof set in ancient Rome and Egypt described as "perhaps the best" of the series.

Indeed...this was the caliber of talent Connor had on *The Land That Time Forgot*.

"We also had a wonderful stunt coordinator," Connor recalled. While he credited Doug McClure as "knowing where to throw a punch for the camera," he praised the stunt staging team of Bill Horrigan, Joe Powell and Colin Skeaping.

"Joe Powell was part of a very famous family of stunt coordinators who also worked on the Bond films. I got a lot of the best people. I was really lucky."

Connor admitted he didn't have clue on fight coordination and left it up to Powell and his team. "He would show me what he rehearsed and I put my two cents in."

The fights were shot in pieces at a time. "It was all handheld with a terrific camera operator, Derek Browne. It's always better handheld for fights. Again, you get the best of the best and they will do it for you."

"I had a great mixture of the old timers and the new guys and I was in the middle. Maurice Carter had these great guys under him who were in the war. Bert Davey was in the war and knew Morse code. So when you see the actors using the lantern to do Morse code in the film that was Davey who was actually doing it. A lot of those guys were in their 20s in the war. You get those guys who have been there and done it, that's why the U33 looked real and authentic."

Connor knew he had a wonderful team of respected engineers and artists and reiterated that he never believed in throwing fits or tantrums on sets to get his people to do things for him. "I can't go by that," he admitted. "I guess I'll never a big top director because I hear that's what they're expected to do. I would rather be myself. I felt I was so lucky to be doing what I wanted to do and working with these talented, knowledgeable people that it never occurred to me to be adversarial. We never had major conflicts on set. By and large, I got on very well with my actors."

I found myself leaving my phone conversations with Connor wishing I worked with him back when he was doing these films. This was the era I should've been directing. He got me excited for a time that no longer exists and made me more determined to get this book finished.

They just don't make 'em like this anymore...

⑦

To Harrison
Continued Success !

THE LAND THAT TIME FORGOT
‾‾‾‾‾‾‾‾‾‾‾‾‾‾‾‾‾‾‾‾‾‾‾‾‾

by

EDGAR RICE BURROUGHS

Screenplay

by

James Cawthorne & Michael Moorcock

* * * *

Best Wishes
Kevin Connor

AMICUS PRODUCTIONS LTD.
Shepperton Studios,
Shepperton, Middx.

Tel: Chertsey 62611
STD: 09328 62611.

Courtesy Kevin Connor

1.

FADE IN:

1. <u>2ND UNIT LOCATION</u>

LONG SHOT SHOOTING UP to a stark rocky clifftop, ugly
against a storm clouded sky. An object is hurled over
the clifftop and the CAMERA PANS (slow motion) with it
as it falls hundreds of feet into the sea.

DISSOLVE TO:

2. <u>2ND UNIT LOCATION</u>

MONTAGE of object (now established as a First World War
Thermos Flask) as it is buffeted amongst ice packs,
whirled around in high seas, etc., until it finally
enters into calmer water.

(This sequence to carry TITLES).

DISSOLVE TO:

3. EXT. CORNISH COAST. DAY. (2ND UNIT LOCATION)

The Lighthouse and cliffs of Land's End are seen with
the sea beating over the rocks in f.g. In the distance
the small figure of a Coast Guard approaches, trudging
across the sand.

4. <u>2ND UNIT LOCATION</u>
(3A.)
M.C.S. COAST GUARD (circa 1918) trudging along. He stops
and looks out to sea. Something in the surf catches his
eye. CAMERA PANS with him as he wades a little way into
the surf and picks up the shell encrusted and thoroughly
battered thermos flask. The COAST GUARD twists open the
top, inspects the interior and pulls out a manuscript.

He unrolls it and begins to read.

We hear over the voice of BOWEN. (This is BOWEN TYLER
looking back on his own experience, aware that his record
will seem incredible, yet desperately anxious to convince
his reader of the truth of his testament.)

                    BOWEN (V.O.)
          I do not expect anyone to believe
          the story I am about to relate. It
          even seems incredible to <u>me</u> that all
          that I have passed through -- all
          those weird and terrifying experiences --
          should have been encompassed within
          so short a span as three brief months.

Courtesy Kevin Connor

Courtesy Kevin Connor

Courtesy Kevin Connor

THE TIMELINE COUNTDOWN

Fortified by plenty of advance production time (pre-production), Connor was ready to take the helm of *The Land That Time Forgot* and get right into the main unit work. "I remember being on that H-Stage and it was freezing cold in early 1974. We had rubber suits on to be in the water so it must've been January-February. They started actual construction work was before Christmas. For the pre-production it was all the main guys but doing second unit."

All of the model shots in the pool, the underwater shots, the plates for the icebergs…all of this was done at Shepperton and done in pre-production. "That was all model work in the same tank. We did the sub escaping from Caprona with the explosions and fire, smoke and stuff like that."

"Derek Meddings was an expert in executing underwater explosions. We were right there in the water alongside the giant model of the sub with everything going off around us as we did that tracking shot."

It was eight full weeks of pre-production and Connor was there for every foot of film shot. Connor lamented the inability to see how things came out instantly like today. Something was shot, then developed and you couldn't see instant playback in 1974 through digital magic.

A key component in smooth shooting is pre-lighting and light rigging and Connor was afforded this. "It was a big set, and with everything pre-lit we could get the shots off, turn around, get another angle without waiting for lighting to be set up."

He praised his art department and special effects team again. "We were like kids having fun doing all of this with things blowing up around you and such."

The German U-boat interiors were the first major scenes of the central unit involving the main actors and the central story. "All of the stuff in the submarine interiors was what we did next after the model and effects shots for second unit."

Main shooting started in January and by April filming moved outside to the back lot. The arrival on the island, meeting the cave tribes, all of that on the back lot. "A few palm trees, some shrubbery and in no time you have a weird new land to make it look it different from the English Countryside. Then we moved off to the sand pit."

Before getting into the timeline of the film and moving through it chronologically (much like the way Connor liked to shoot whenever possible), I asked about the violence factor of the film.

"I was never much for blood and gore. It was kid's stuff. You can also move quicker without blood bursts and bag bursts because all of that takes time." Connor did go on to repeat his focus on the action with the stunts, fighting and his excellent fight coordinators.

"None of the stunts were particularly complicated. I had had a wonderful camera operator though who knew where the punches would land and Doug was involved in his fights and contributed his own action and worked with the stunt guys who loved him. He knew how to punch for the camera. Doug was always spot on."

McClure knew where the camera was and knew how to line up his punch as if he had eyes in the back of his head.

The opening of the film was shot on The Isle of Skye and once moving into the sub interiors after the terrifically inventive steamer sinking the main film unfolds.

Connor offered his very practical assessment of Doug McClure since he was by far the biggest name in the film. There were no salacious stories of the actor and Connor avoided hyperbole. Every step of the way in my interviews he reiterated what a pleasure it was to work with McClure and what good friends they became.

The fight on the sub exterior and then the later frigid polar shots were all done on H-Stage with a full size build in the giant tank. Waves were created by technicians with paddles off camera giving the ocean surface its constant movement.

The interiors were approved by a real German U-boat captain and Connor was able to get all he needed in the tight quarters. "Doug had to operate a real periscope but it couldn't go all the way up because of hitting the roof of the cave in the film, but it actually went up and down a bit for that realism."

Connor took credit for the shot that came with the periscope, a terrific jump scare as McClure peers through the lens and gets a 3-D type of strike from a water dinosaur laying in wait, attacking the sub like a cobra.

"I just wanted something, you know? Just a blur or blob, something we can just push in front of the camera suddenly."

It worked and I remember it giving me one hell of a start in theaters.

"That was just something I grabbed at that moment while we were shooting. It wasn't storyboarded. That is the magic of it all… those little moments. I had to have a scary shot, you know?"

What makes it work even better is that the shot is done without sound. When the beast lurches from the water, it's silent because McClure and crew were all underwater and couldn't hear anything out there. It still works.

THE ERA THAT TIME FORGOT • 169

The photo of the boat trick used in sinking the steamer was used again later when McClure and his team flash an SOS to a British warship only to be fired on. The ship that you see firing on the U-boat is not a model, but once again a photo of a period ship taken from a British model in a glass show-case at the entrance to the Shepperton Studioo offices.

If something works, you stick with it. For all these years I thought both ships were models, with the second one definitely being one. I was wrong. Way wrong.

Underwater cameras were deployed for the entry into Caprona, tracking the sub along the ocean bottom. A large tunnel was built for the miniature set that the sub would track along before surfacing on the other side of the ice barrier. Matte paintings for the sub's descent into the fresh water river were used behind the iceberg sets.

"All those shots they built an underwater tunnel that we could get in front or behind the sub with a bright light. The light on the submarine would also light up which would give a great effect for the dirty water, the weeds, and the debris floating in it."

Connor pushed Derek Meddings to make sure the sub hit an underwater bend constructed in the tunnel. He wanted that show the treacherous move through the passage and a terrific clunk of sound comes with this when the sub strikes the rocky bend, adding to the tension.

"We shot 32 frames to slow it down a bit," Connor said. "It all worked, especially when the sound effects were added by a wonderfully creative sound designer, Don Sharpe."

The dinosaurs were all around four or five feet tall, operated very much like Muppets with hands and rods and sticks to get the movement needed.

The full-sized dinosaur was the flying reptile that swoops down on McClure for Ahm the caveman to step in and save his friend, scooped up in the creature's jaws and flown away.

"That was a full-sized model attached to a crane," Connor said. "This crane driver thought we were all bonkers because he had never seen anything like it. After a bit though, he really liked and how he could make this thing move by making the crane swing was fantastic."

The crane driver got into it with the crew. He was good at making the reptile hit its marks every time with such precision. "Unfortunately you can see the wires in some shots," Connor lamented.

The attack on Ahm was done in a series of shots all cut together. The reptile was shot coming down, swooping into frame. Then the actor playing Ahm would move himself to meet the large prop, to make it look like the inflexible model was actually scooping him up.

"We'd get all that, then Doug would come in on the next shot, you know, about ten times at different angles. We shot it on two handheld cameras for that one I think because you never know what you're gonna get. You only need like ten frames or so but you needed to shoot a lot to get that."

A model reptile was used for the distant shot with a model Ahm in its jaws, flying away. The miniature work is terrific and without a stitch of CG.

"Our Mososaurus was also a full-sized beast but a bit droopy, if you will," Connor chuckled. A crew operated from it above and to the sides, moving the massive head to make it strike at McClure and the other actor on the com bridge of the sub. The issue with this scene is the scale between the puppet dinosaur and the full-sized one don't really match up. The full creature looks smaller than the shots of it as a puppet.

"It was very hard to get this thing to come down in one swoop, and that took a little while to get." Connor laughed at remembering the ordeal to get those shots.

Did Connor ever consider different dinosaur effects while shooting, such as Suitmation? There was no real budget for shifting or upgrading. "It was such a tight budget," he said. "It didn't occur to me to ask for anything like that. You're trained to be responsible to make this film for the money they gave you and that was it. You didn't think of asking for more. Maybe another camera or something but nothing in the way of changing effects or changing them up while filming."

What Connor loved and repeated was that the puppets allowed such terrific close-ups for the detail they afforded. "I was blessed with top people and I think that's what gave such unique style and look to my films because I had such great people and things stayed consistent from film to film."

There was one thing that always perplexed me, even as a boy and I asked Connor for any insight. Once the team arrives on land, they construct a small crude oil refinery to create fuel for the trip back home.

They find the crude in these pools but when we see the makeshift refinery at the base camp, in the background runs this giant wooden fence. The logs are sharpened into points as if to keep something out.

Ahm is shown hacking away at logs, which I assume was to add to the barrier the humans created to keep dinosaurs from trouncing their little refinery. My question was…did Connor shoot anything that got cut showing a dinosaur attack on the base camp?

If not, then why was this giant set constructed? It seemed like an expense to make and it wasn't a matte painting. Exactly why was it there?

"I don't know," Connor admitted. "They built it on the Shepperton back lot." They did not shoot anything with the fence or any kind of scene at the refinery area. The fence was just there. perhaps it just looked good, but that giant fencing or wall reminded me of *King Kong* and the wall created to keep the go-ape in the jungle.

"You know, it might have been a pre-existing set that art department and production design teams thought would look good and they used it. I don't know," Connor said.

That explanation would make much more sense from a budgetary perspective.

Mystery Science Theater pointed out something important about the film toward its end. When the volcano erupts and Caprona starts to fall apart, Doug McClure and Susan Penhaligon run for their lives for the submarine after escaping the villain cave tribe camp.

They run along large pools of crude oil. I asked Connor before I got to the *Mystery Science Theater* topic; just what did they use for crude oil. They couldn't have used real oil, could they?

"It was real oil," Connor told me. "This was all part of the sand pit location. "That's what we used in those days. The quicksand stuff that McClure and Susan fell into was just murky water."

Real oil…then this underscores what *Mystery Science Theater* observed in their rift episode on the film. Doug and Susan are running with real fire falling around them!

There was no CGI at that time, so were they really throwing globs or pieces of burning shit at the two actors?

Yes.

"They were large pieces of Styrofoam dipped in a grease. We had eight guys lobbing stuff in as they ran through. I mean we had to be careful where they threw it and Doug was good at navigating Susan..."

Holy shit!

Eight people chucking a crude form of Napalm at the lead talent. Today that would be a liability nightmare. Connor laughed at it all, his casual demeanor assuring me it wasn't as big of a deal as I made it out to be.

Mystery Science Theater thought it might be, reminding the audience that those were real people winding their way through fire thrown at them.

"The real drawback," Connor went on to say, "Was that the pieces were so light they would bounce. That was a problem because they're supposed to be these heavy pieces of molten rock and sometimes they hit the ground and bounced like rubber balls."

Watch it for yourself. That's real fire chucked at those two actors.

"We used some library stock shots of volcano eruptions of course. We just did it. There was a lot of good material available to us. It was all real shots of a volcano; we didn't do any miniature work with that."

Caprona erupts; McClure and Susan stand on the riverbank and watch the doomed sub head back toward the tunnel. While marooned on the burning continent, they fared better than the U-boat crew who all perish just at the mouth of the exit and sink to fiery deaths.

Do all the dinosaurs die? Will McClure live? What about all those evil cave people out there and the concept that they were evolving too?

Lots of questions form at the end, maybe even more than when the team arrived.

We end the film with those double actors walking the snow on the Isle of Skye and the hurling the yellow canister into the water with McClure's story inside.

But the story isn't over. Burroughs wrote a sequel.

Almost three years later my mother got a phone call from my aunt asking if my brother and I wanted to go to the drive-in that summer night with my cousins to see a double header feature: *The People That Time Forgot* and *At the Earth's Core*.

Wait...*The People That Time Forgot*? Could that be related to *The Land That Time Forgot*? This was before I could palm a phone and tap into any entertainment news database to get the answer in seconds.

This was before sequel-mania erupted with *Jaws 2* a year later.

People WAS a sequel to that kickass dinosaur movie my father took to me to see a few year earlier. Yes! Hell yes we wanted to go.

My mother made the plans and drove us from East Bangor to Mt. Pocono where my aunt and uncle and cousin packed into a 1974 *Thunderbird* and headed out to *Eagle Valley Drive-In* in East Stroudsburg, Pennsylvania to see the double dino bill.

I would move to neighboring Stroudsburg a year later.

Movies were great.

=. 10   CUT OUT — TANK
           & PERISCOPE MASK

Sc 11.   STUDIO SET.

2   STO. K

Sc. 13   CUT OUT. TANK

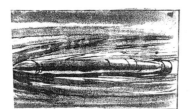

        MODEL   15

              INT. SUB. SET

Courtesy Kevin Connor

11.

32. <u>INT. FOREPART OF INT. CONNING-TOWER. DAY.</u> (Tank. Fog.)

VON SCHOENVORTS, calm and defiant in the face of the excited BENSON, spreads his fingers towards the action alarm signal button.

33. <u>SIGNAL BUTTON</u>

CLOSE ON VON SCHOENVORTS' fingers as he presses.

34. <u>INT. CONNING-TOWER U-33. DAY.</u> (Tank. Fog.)

The siren shrieks out and BOWEN swings round and knocks SMITH's arm down as he fires at VON SCHOENVORTS. Then everything happens.

35. <u>EXT. DECK OF U-33. DAY.</u> (Tank. Fog.)

The gunners' hatch on the deck bursts open and PLESSER throws himself through it firing as he comes. PLESSER has no time to turn before he is clubbed down by OLSON whose attention has been distracted from the hatch only a moment by the strident sound of the siren. SMITH is shot as he climbs down the Conning-Tower.

35A. <u>EXT. SEA. LIFEBOAT.</u> (Tank)

In the boat, LISA sees PLESSER's gun bounce from the deck and skid across the curve of the pressure hull. LISA grabs the gun just before it hits the water.

35B. <u>EXT. DECK OF U-33. DAWN.</u>

The struggle spreads out along the deck. WHITELEY, OLSON and BOWEN fight a group of GERMANS. They are now on the narrow deck-area at one side of the Conning-Tower, almost directly above the boat. BOWEN is fighting a GERMAN armed with a rifle. A burst of gun-fire in the Conning-Tower. A dead GERMAN SAILOR plunges to the deck, sending BOWEN staggering. His opponent swings the rifle-butt. BOWEN shields his head with his arms, but the impact of the blow drives him against the rail. Half over the rail, momentarily dazed, he sees the rifle swinging at him again. Then a shot rings out. The GERMAN yells and falls back dead, his rifle clattering across the deck.

Courtesy Kevin Connor

9

FOG - TANK.

35
FOG - TANK

A
FOG - TANK

35B
FOG - TANK

C
FOG - TANK

36
INT. SUB. SET

Courtesy Kevin Connor

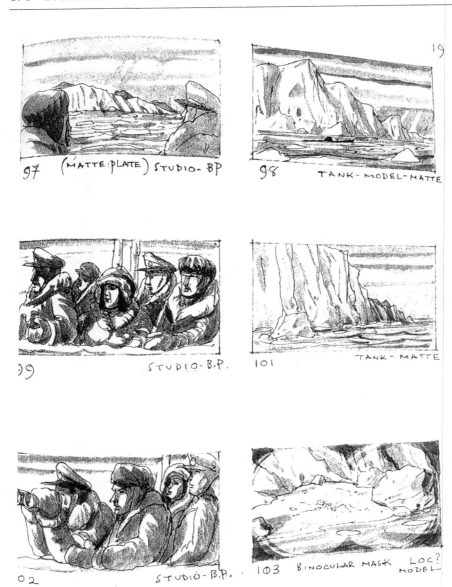

Courtesy Kevin Connor

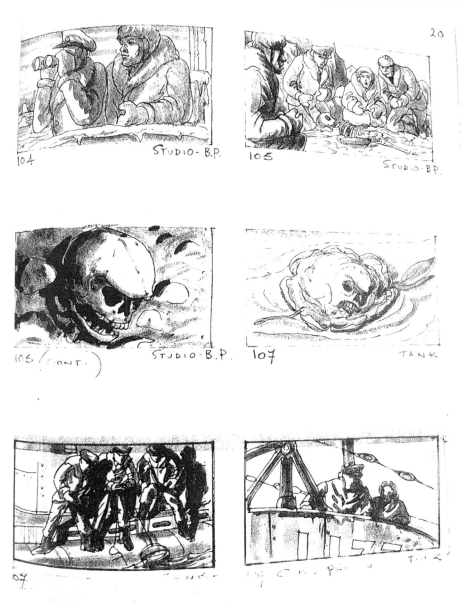

Courtesy Kevin Connor

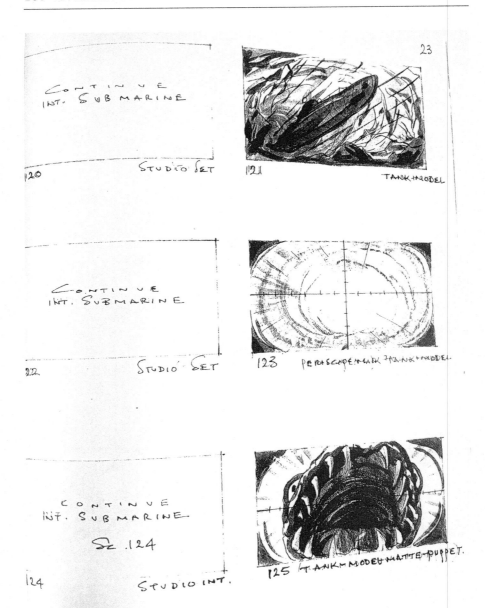

CONTINUE
INT. SUBMARINE

120   STUDIO SET   121   TANK+MODEL

23

CONTINUE
INT. SUBMARINE

122   STUDIO SET   123   PERISCOPE MARK 7 TANK+MODEL

CONTINUE
INT. SUBMARINE

Sc .124

124   STUDIO INT.   125 TANK+MODEL MATTE+PUPPET.

Courtesy Kevin Connor

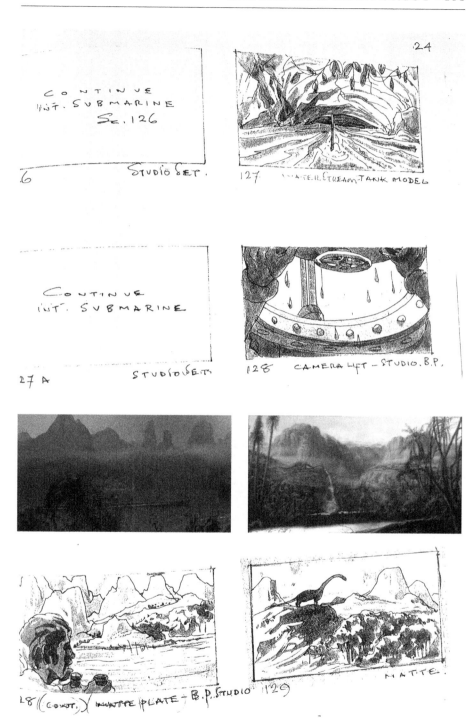

Courtesy Kevin Connor

44.

151. INT. MODEL CONNING-TOWER. U-33. DAY. (BP. Matte Plate)

The PLESIOSAURUS withdraws its head and then gains height with its neck ready to lunge and able to reach BOWEN hissing horribly.

152. EXT./INT. CONNING-TOWER. U-33. DAY. (BP. Matte Plate)

OLSON shakes his head and disappears hurriedly below.

153. EXT./INT. CONNING-TOWER. U-33.

REVERSE with BP. PLATE OF MODEL. Over shoulder of BOWEN.

The PLESIOSAURUS makes a lunge, but is defeated by the hatch cover.

154. EXT./INT. CONNING-TOWER. U-33. DAY. (BP. Matte Plate)

Onto BOWEN looking over CAMERA.

BOWEN fires four or five shots very fast.

155. EXT. MODEL CONNING-TOWER. U-33. DAY. (Sky backing)

The PLESIOSAURUS ready for another lunge is slightly halted as teeth fly and blood flows from its wounds, but they are only pinpricks.

156. EXT./INT. CONNING-TOWER. U-33. DAY. (BP. Matte Plate)

With a roar it lunges through shot again and BOWEN fires point blank at it.

157. EXT. MODEL CONNING-TOWER. U-33. DAY. (Sky backing)

Blood streams from the beast, but it is unaffected and screams with rage, ready to make the final attack.

Courtesy Kevin Connor

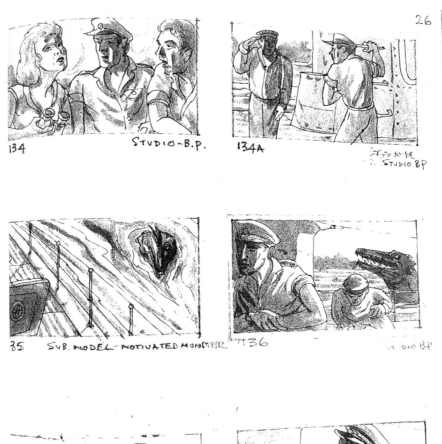

Courtesy Kevin Connor

5   MODEL PLATE - STUDIO·B.P.

28

146   TANK PLATE - STUDIO B.P.

47   MODEL & PUPPET

148   TANK PLATE   STUDIO·B.P.

49   MODEL & PUPPET

150   FULL-SIZE HEAD - STUDIO B.P.

Courtesy Kevin Connor

55

259

TANK-MODEL

STUDIO-B.P.

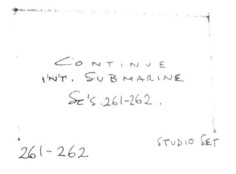

CONTINUE
INT. SUBMARINE
Sc's. 261-262.

261-262

STUDIO SET

TANK-MODEL

264

LOC.

Courtesy Kevin Connor

Courtesy Kevin Connor

(CONT)   LOC

34

179 (CONT)   LOC.

PUPPETS & MODEL

181   LOC.

PUPPETS & MODEL

183   LOC

Courtesy Kevin Connor

Courtesy Kevin Connor

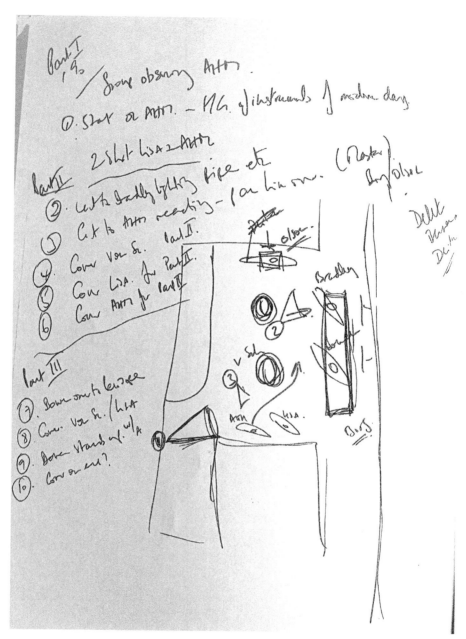

Connor's notes for choreography and actor
placement included with his storyboards.

Courtesy Kevin Connor

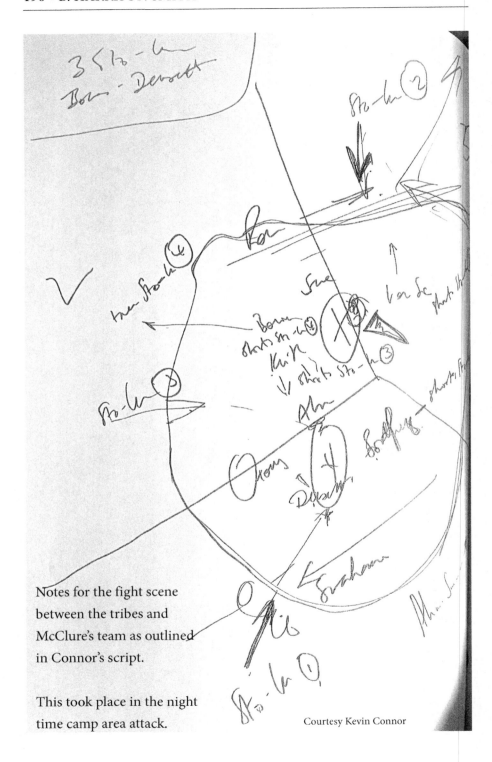

Notes for the fight scene
between the tribes and
McClure's team as outlined
in Connor's script.

This took place in the night
time camp area attack.

Courtesy Kevin Connor

Courtesy Kevin Connor

LISA: This must be a Sto — the encampment.

HOLDEN:
DOUG: Look at the women in that Pool!
Sset !!

LISA: That must be how life begins in Capung
That's the secret of Caprona?

HOLDEN: What are they doing?

LISA: You remember the samples we took from
the river — and the spawn we saw
under the microscope. —

BOWEN: You mean to tell me that they're laying
eggs.

or Capronia

LISA: Yes every creature must lay eggs in the
They flow into the rivers and develop thru
every stage of evolution.

Courtesy Kevin Connor

ATM

1. Bird swoops over — and away.
2. ATM knocked over — Reverse.
3. Doug sits up + reacts.
4. ATM sitting up + picks up axe.
5. Bird swoops.
6. Doug stands up + pauses
7. Bird swoops.
8. ATM turns.
*9. — Birds Beak comments
10. — Doug nuts
12. — Bird takes off with ATM.
13. — Doug run
14. — Bird + ATM.
15. — Doug reaches for ATM
16. — ATM P.O.V. on Doug.
17. — Bird over ____ cliff.
18. — Doug stops and looks — c.s.
19. — L.S. Bird flying away.

Doug — looks away
calls — Denson
— while
hears Lx +
exits

Courtesy Kevin Connor

Courtesy Kevin Connor

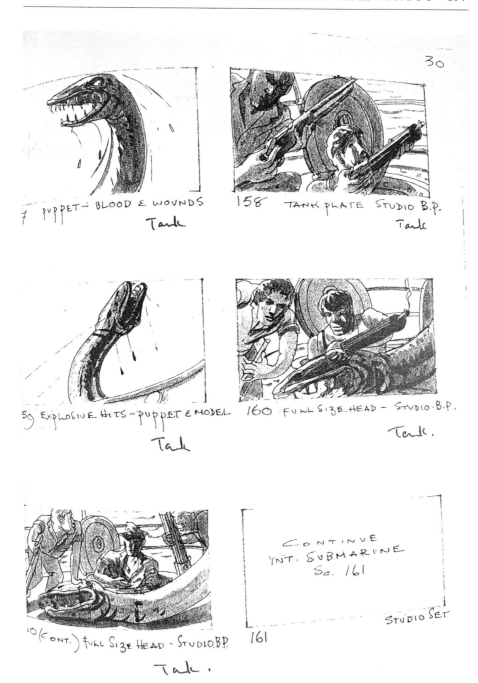

7 PUPPET - BLOOD & WOUNDS
Tank

158 TANK PLATE STUDIO B.P.
Tank

59 EXPLOSIVE HITS - PUPPET & MODEL
Tank

160 FULL SIZE HEAD - STUDIO B.P.
Tank.

°0 (CONT.) FULL SIZE HEAD - STUDIO BP.
Tank.

161

CONTINUE
INT. SUBMARINE
Sc. 161

STUDIO SET

Courtesy Kevin Connor

Courtesy Kevin Connor

88.

265. EXT. PLAINS OF CAPRONA

Two lonely figures walking across the landscape.

DISSOLVE:

266. EXT. VAST LAND MASS OF CAPRONA

Two lonely figures.

DISSOLVE:

267. EXT. MOUNTAINSIDE ON CAPRONA

Two lonely figures climbing.

DISSOLVE:

268. DELETED.

269. EXT. TOP OF CLIFFS. SUN-SET. (LOCATION. BP. SEA PLATE)

It is evening. The sun reddens the sky. BOWEN and LISA stand hand in hand. He holds the thermos flask and detaching himself from LISA, throws it far out over and into the sea.

BOWEN'S COMMENTARY

"With the sinking of the submarine all our hopes of ever getting away from Caprona have disappeared. We are alone - spurned by even the highest - the Galu. So we have to go on - in the way life-style of Caprona till we find peace. Well, it might be worse. I would rather live here with Lisa than to live elsewhere without her; and she says the same of me.

Tonight the clouds broke, and the sun shone down upon us; and there, hand in hand, we turned our faces toward heaven and plighted our troth beneath the eyes of God. No human agency could have married us more sacredly than we are wed. We are man and wife, and we are content. If God wills it, we shall live our lives here. However, we are determined to move ever northward, ever forward, toward the greater mysteries that lie ahead. And so we say goodbye in this, our last message to the world beyond the barrier cliffs - of this land that time forgot.

270. EXT. CAPRONA CLIFFS. (REPEAT OF SCENE 1)

The thermos flask comes hurtling over the cliff and the CAMERA PANS (SLOW MOTION) with it as it falls hundreds of feet into the boiling sea.

MUSIC SWELLS UP.

271. END TITLES CARRIED OVER MONTAGE OF THERMOS FLASK. (SCENES 2B and 3A)

THE END

Courtesy Kevin Connor

41B.
(Old
59)

INT. VON SCHOENVORTS' CABIN. U-33. (STUDIO)

As VON SCHOENVORTS walks in, OLSON casually puts one large
foot on the threshold, making it impossible to close the
door. The cabin is tiny, with three vertical sides formed
by bulkheads, the fourth a curved segment of the hull.
Books in several languages are jammed into every space,
and prominent amongst them is a copy of THE ORIGIN OF THE
SPECIES by Charles Darwin. A microscope case, in brass
and mahogany, is secured to a shelf. A bunk occupies
most of the floor area.

VON SCHOENVORTS begins to sort through a rack of
navigational charts.

                    VON SCHOENVORTS
              Your Mr. Tyler has decided to
              take us all to England. I find
              his Yankee ingenuousness almost
              frightening.

VON SCHOENVORTS, sorting charts, does not see LISA check
a flare of anger. She replies almost defensively, almost
inconsequentially.

                    LISA
              He saved my life!

VON SCHOENVORTS straightens up and turns to face her, an
open chart in his hands.

                    VON SCHOENVORTS
                   (charmingly)
              Then we are all in Mr. Tyler's
              debt.
                 I'm glad to see you making yourself at home
LISA looks at VON SCHOENVORTS without resentment. She
gestures to the stacked books and notebooks.

                    LISA
                   (slowly)
              I'm a biologist, Captain von Schoenvorts.
              I study not only the structure of
              living things but their behaviour
              and motivations. But I don't under-
              stand you, how can anyone who's interested in life
              deep an interest in natural philosophy,
              in the growth and order of life, follow
              a profession devoted to killing and
              destruction?

LISA's question is almost amusing to VON SCHOENVORTS,
though the amusement seems tinged with despair. He
is not laughing at her, just at the question itself.

Courtesy Kevin Connor

ace SCIENCE FICTION CLASSIC F-220 40¢

EDGAR RICE BURROUGHS

THE PEOPLE THAT TIME FORGOT

Trapped between the primitive and the unknown

PART II

THE PEOPLE THAT TIME FORGOT

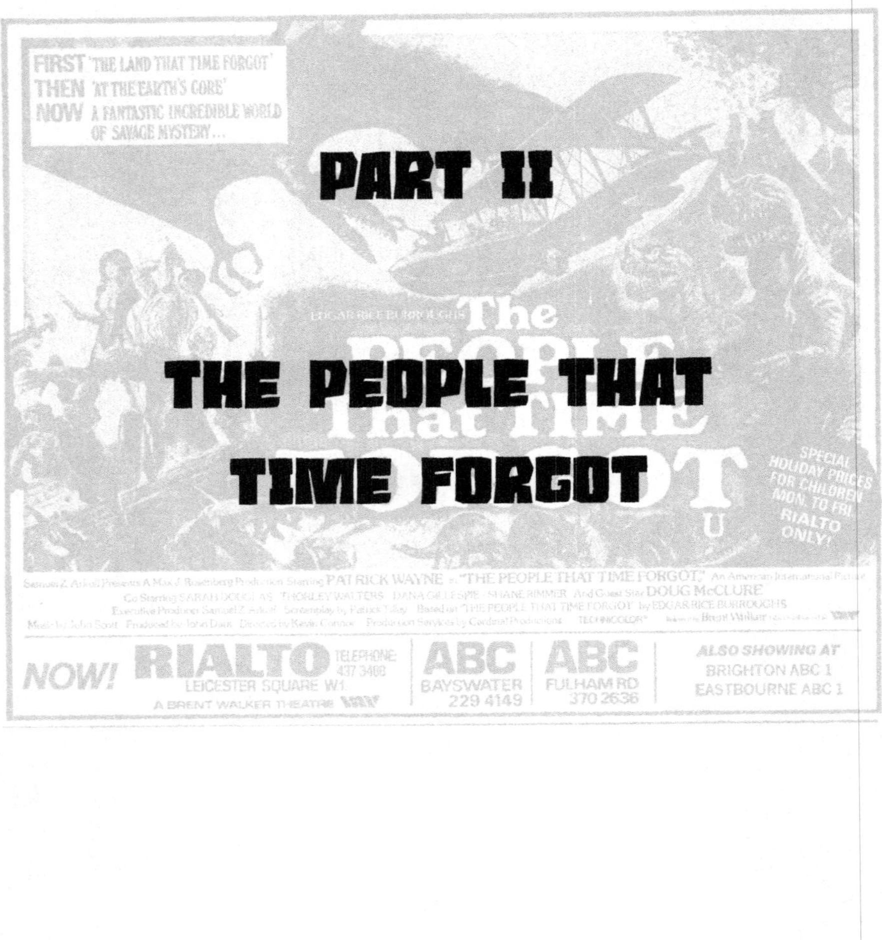

SEQUELS...

1977 was the year *Star Wars* dropped and added to the chain reaction caused by Spielberg's *Jaws* just two years earlier. Both films would not only change the way films were released (*Jaws* being the first summer blockbuster); they would have a profound impact on how audiences viewed special effects.

They would also take away the stigma of the word "sequel" and redefine the word "franchise." *Jaws* had hardly any "visual effects." There was no blue screen or front or rear projection. The shark was a giant mechanical prop. There was no CGI and no miniatures.

Jaws gave us visceral entertainment—from its location on the real and rough Atlantic Ocean to genuine New England towns and coast lines, *Jaws* offered authenticity as part of its effects lineup.

Aside from a few underwater segments shot on the Universal lot in a tank or editor Verna Fields' back yard pool, Spielberg opted for genuine locations to bring the story to life and make the film an immersive experience.

Its sequel would not follow this track.

Star Wars gave us an even bigger "Wow Factor." While blue screen technology had been around for at least a decade, the model work, the computerized camera control with effects supervisor John Dykstra at the helm not only raised the bar for special effects, it also raised audience expectations.

Perhaps the term "dated" started here. With these new, spectacular effects, audiences found out what they were missing. Classic

204 • B. HARRISON SMITH

films from the 50s and 60s save for Kubrick's *2001* suddenly looked campy and amateurish.

Star Wars popularized what Kubrick put into motion with his groundbreaking film. *Star Wars* built the block buster around special effects and helped it evolve.

Even 1976's *King Kong* looked a bit silly in comparison to X-wing and Tie Fighter battles, creature cantinas and exploding Death Stars. The giant robot ape that made less than 30 seconds in the final cut was big, expensive and hokey.

1977 was the ride up the roller coaster and the 80s would be the drop and one long looping thrill ride through the era of new effects that would take us into the digital revolution.

1976 saw the network screening of *Godzilla vs. Megalon*. The venerated radioactive lizard had been with Americans since the 1955 American cut of *Gojira* re-titled *Godzilla: King of the Monsters*.

The Japanese monster film was taken out of context in its American run and as sequels lined up they gained a reputation for campy, low brow men in suits romps. They were the stuff of drive-in double bills and eventually Saturday afternoon creature feature lineups.

NBC decided to have some fun with all of it and in 1976 chose what might be the worst of all of the films, to debut on national, prime television hosted by none other than Not Ready For Prime Time *Saturday Night Live* star, John Belushi. The show was a smash hit and only one year into its still going run.

Belushi, a Godzilla fan, donned a ratty, silly Godzilla suit and gave the movie a *Mystery Science Theater* riffing long before that show came about.

With the white hot stardom of Belushi on the nation's most popular TV show at that time, *Godzilla vs. Megalon* got exposure usually reserved for high profile blockbuster movies for network premiers.

Of all the Godzilla films to that time, this was perhaps the worst example to show American audiences. By this time the series had degenerated into little kid matinee fluff. It was professional wrestling with monster suits. The stories had gone off the rails with alien invasions, magic growing robots, and talking monsters.

The Godzilla suit was among the worst—with Godzilla losing his once fearsome appearance like in the days of 1963's *King Kong vs. Godzilla* (arguably the fan favorite of all Godzilla suits) and taking on a more Muppet, feline appearance.

With exception of a terrific outdoor miniature effects shot of Megalon plowing through a hydroelectric dam, the effects were laughable with many shots re-used from previous movies to save on the budgets (which had been dwindling for years).

Godzilla was already one year into retirement, closing out the Showa series of films with 1975's *Terror of Mecha Godzilla* and Toho Studios decided to give the Big Guy a long-deserved break.

Belushi's hosting of *Godzilla vs. Megalon* burned in the concept of Godzilla and big monster movies as Grade Z entertainment to be mocked and derided. The bad lip-syncing, the cheap model effects and silly stories were embodied by *Godzilla vs. Megalon* and given a huge platform in America.

This solidified the already forming consensus that giant monster movies were light-hearted kid fare and nothing more. Belushi turned it into *Rocky Horror*.

For me, whatever ground Kevin Connor made in the original *Land That Time Forgot* was lost a bit because of this and the changing perception of giant monster and dinosaur films.

By 1977, the tide had turned against big monsters and replaced with the intense action of *Jaws* and the dynamic effects of *Star Wars*.

Did Connor get this? He knew his audience. He knew there was a market out there for these kind of films and the box office returns proved that. He did not change course.

The time between The *Land That Time Forgot* and *The People That Time Forgot* produced *At the Earth's Core*, again featuring Doug McClure and co-starring a *Star Wars* name with Peter Cushing.

Cushing was introduced to a whole new legion of young fans thanks to *Star Wars* and *Core* could be argued to be the last of his old monster, Hammer years before being known thereafter as Governor Tarkin, chief of Death Star operations.

The People That Time Forgot dropped summer, 1977 as part of a double drive-in bill with *At the Earth's Core*. Connor's ability to make these films back to back came from the ability to roll his stellar crew into one film right after the other.

People is a sequel to *Land* in the Burroughs books as well, but while *Land* stayed close to its source material, *People* will diverge from it, although I argue *People* might be the more ambitious of the two films.

What is a sequel, exactly? Today the term is clouded by "reboot" or "remakes." The word was once a pretty clear thing: a continuation of the original story. Sometimes some of the main characters from the previous film came along for the ride or at least had a cameo to show continuity in the series.

Sequels go back to the silent era and with monsters and horror, they became popular and laid the foundation for world building and extended universes.

While *Son of Kong* failed to blow up the boxoffice like its 1933 predecessor, films like *The Bride of Frankenstein* showed how a sequel could possibly eclipse the original film in terms of quality and story.

Movie theaters ran "serials", episodic adventures of characters whether super heroes of science fiction ones, but they weren't true feature films. They were shorts that ran before the major film you paid to see.

However *The Thin Man* was a non-monster, horror series with numerous sequels and other films also had their installments. Sequel was not an original thing by 1977, but it was a tarnished word in most corners of studio offices.

The Universal Monsters took "sequel" and ran with it. By start of World War II, Universal was pairing up its famous monsters with one another in ways Godzilla would pattern after later. *Frankenstein Meets the Wolfman*, or *House of Dracula, House of Frankenstein* saw compiling these monsters, long facing reduced boxoffice on their own, with other fading monster stars and curiosity and novelty brought out fans to see their favorites monsters fight each other.

Abbott and Costello Meet Frankenstein might be the best example of this and the gateway for many Gen X'ers into the world of horror. We will see *New Line Cinema* and *Paramount Pictures* do this with limited success with *Freddy vs. Jason* which was really nothing more than an R-rated *Frankenstein Meets the Wolfman* type of setup.

The point is, these were all true sequels. They might have switched out actors here and there but the stories were all connected and a kind of official "canon."

Today the line is a bit more blurred. Look at the *Halloween* films starting with the 1978 original and then move forward to the 2018 "sequel" which also is a kind of reboot. The filmmakers go back, expunge 1981's true sequel, *Halloween II* from the timeline. They ignore the events of *Halloween H20* and its dismal *Resurrection* follow up. Jamie Lee Curtis died in the opening of the "Tyra Banks *Halloween*" movie.

All of this was ignored and yet, *Halloween III: Season of the Witch*, a sequel never meant to be a direct sequel to the 1978 or 1981 film somehow is part of the 2018 world.

Confusing? You bet. That's because it's a damned mess and that "sequel/reboot/remake" spawned two more lousier films with *Halloween Kills* and *Halloween Ends* and closed out (for the time being) the Haddonfield storyline.

Jaws 2 is credited with bringing the shine to the word sequel. When you make *Jaws* and it rakes in 100 million in less than six weeks, someone is going to want more. Sharks make money and there had to be more than one big shark in the ocean.

There was and Universal went back to *Jaws* director Steven Spielberg with a blank check to make a sequel. When Spielberg balked, calling sequels "Cheap carnival tricks" he briefly played along and banged out a "prequel" script that focused on Quint's World War II story of the sinking of the *USS Indianapolis* and the shark feeding frenzy that Quint survived and fueled his hatred for the animals.

Universal turned it down (I think Spielberg knew they would, giving him an easy out) and opted for continuing the Amity Island story with Chief Brody.

After strong-arming a kicking and screaming Roy Scheider to return to the role, they tried to capture lighting in a bottle again with a unknown director. John Hancock was brought on after making a nifty, atmospheric horror film, *Let's Scare Jessica to Death* in 1976.

Hancock had a dark vision for the film. It would be murky, misty, blue and show the economic impact of the first shark attacks on Amity. The town was now decrepit and suffering under economic collapse and then—another shark showed up.

Universal canned Hancock roughly six weeks into production for a number of reasons; with the main one being his dark vision didn't match the studio's.

The studio wanted big screen, rich, bright colors, blue sky, sun and action. Hancock was replaced by a team player director, the script was re-written and the entire production rebooted to give us what we got in the summer of 1978.

The film had one of the most brilliant taglines in film history, "Just when you thought it was safe to go back into the water…"

It all worked. Sharkmania was back and while the film didn't do the numbers of the original, it kicked boxoffice ass and for awhile was the number one grossing sequel of all time.

The success of *Jaws 2* showed sequels can not only make money, they can make BIG money for a long timer—as long as studios can get away with it.

As a result horror franchises followed suit—*Halloween*, *Friday the 13th* and more ran up the Roman numerals behind their original titles and new worlds were created.

By the mid-1980s, it was almost expected for any original film to have some kind of franchise potential. 80s film is almost solely defined by sequels from horror through big-budget, A-list series.

Connor saw the potential in worlds and franchises. He saw the potential of not just *The Land That Time Forgot* franchise but also Burroughs's *John Carter of Mars* series.

The problem was the Burroughs estate also saw potential and their prices to license the materials became more and more problematic.

At the Earth's Core was a small veering but Connor came right back to Caprona with *The People That Time Forgot.* All of this was a year before *Jaws 2* would turn things around for sequels.

I was excited to see the film, and again on a big screen. The memories of *The Land That Time Forgot* were

Cinematreasures.org

still fresh and exciting. What would this one be? I didn't see Doug McClure in the trailer (or did I?). What would happen in those? I thought the island blew up at the end of the first one.

There were more dinosaurs, so the big lizards lived. There was snow, ice and some kind of pre-*Temple of Doom* cave type lair. Giant snakes were crashing out of rock walls.

Yeah…this was the stuff I wanted to see. This was what got me excited.

My mother relayed the question from her sister if I would like to see the movie at the drive-in up by her in the Poconos.

My answer was a resounding: "YES!"

MGM Studios

AN AMBITIOUS SEQUEL

A good sequel takes the original story and builds upon it, taking the viewer/reader into a new adventure without rehashing the original one. There is also the temptation to use flashbacks in sequels to the original film and for the most part, they backfire, often reminding us of just how much better the original film was.

1986's *Poltergeist II* showed this well.

There is nothing inherently wrong with sequels. Roy Scheider bit the bullet with *Jaws 2* and told onset reporter, Ray Lloynd for *The Jaws 2 Log*, that there was nothing wrong with bringing back a story if it gives people a good time. He cited Sherlock Holmes as an example.

Scheider wasn't wrong.

Jaws 2's only crime was that it was not *Jaws* and Universal tried to give the audience so much of the same that some critics called the film a "retread" of the original.

Connor moved *People* into some new territory. Gone would be the war storyline and the camaraderie of rivals. Instead we have a rescue mission for McClure's character. We know his canister was found and turns out his childhood best friend got some people to fund a rescue mission to Caprona.

We have a colorful cast of characters, with another smart lead female star with Sarah Douglas, just on the eve of major worldwide fame playing super villain Ursa in *Superman II* just a few years later.

Gifted with a few more bucks for this film, Connor made good use of it. This time around we get right into the story and we see dinosaurs far sooner than we did in *Land*.

A lost continent of dinosaurs and prehistoric humanoids…what else could you possibly do without rehashing the same story over?

Connor answered that question confidently. The script focused more on the mythos of the island and the weird human story at its center atop a mountain outfitted with a skull castle fitting for any Frank Frazetta fan.

There's a lot to unpack with *The People That Time Forgot*. Connor is more relaxed in his directing this time around, allowing certain set pieces to unfold a little longer, allowing his camera to stay on things a bit more than the first time around.

Connor embraces action in this film, with some aerial stunts and dinosaur fights and then heading into *Conan the Barbarian* territory by the end of the film.

We know we are in for something different this time around just by the opening credit sequence.

Instead of a wide seascape Connor gave us blackened, volcanic soil, stripped trees and a hard, dark misty landscape. In some ways it has the tone and feel of what *Jaws 2* would've had under John Hancock.

Are we seeing the aftermath of the desolation from the first film? Did the volcano strip everything down and it's all regrowing? There is no bright sun, blue skies…instead a volcanic landscape shrouded by mist and fog.

It is eerie and as a boy I knew I was in for a very different story.

The entire film would be shot in the Canary Islands this time around. No back Shepperton lot, no sand pit, but rather this unique tropical and arid landscape located off of northwestern Africa.

Behind the scenes, *Amicus* was going through what Connor described as a "Boardroom Battle" that resulted in the company splitting and Milton Subotsky taking the title of the company and heading off on his own from Max Rosenberg and John Dark.

"Milton never liked John Dark at all, and that's what happened. We did *At the Earth's Core* and then *People* popped up and I thought, Well, why not?" "

It was a natural progression from *Core* to *People* and Connor was unsure exactly how the film came to be but it was the next one to come up and off they went.

"It was a great atmosphere between everyone making these films. So I was always happy to return to these films. I did some films in between *Land* and *People*. It looked like we were going to get the same team back again so I was happy to return."

The pre-production process was similar to *Land*. "We had almost exactly the same crew again. Carter, Hume, Meddings and all those guys. I wasn't crazy about the first script I read and I had a go at it but nobody really liked it, although I did."

Patrick Tilley got credit for the final script. Connor thought he was a terrific guy and just had his own ideas for the story, but in the end the studio went with Tilley's script.

"There was one particular island of the Canary Islands that had this deep, dark black soil which gave it an eerie look. We went there and loaded up a plane—crew, props, actors and flew out of England to the islands to unload, set up and welcomed by the mayor and township."

There was studio work was shot back at Pinewood Studios without about 40% of the film shot on location in the islands.

"We didn't build anything on the islands. It was really about the plane, and the plane landing. We got some aerial shots for plates when the plane flies in. The model landing and shots were all done on a stage at Pinewood."

The production was on island about three weeks. I asked about those opening titles. "There was this range of mountains and dark hills all around us and I said to grab a second camera and these foreboding hills and mountains look like a great title background," Connor told me.

Connor's instincts were spot on because the moody feel of those titles hit me as a boy and set an entirely different tone.

"It's much darker," Connor confirmed. "They're on adventure to find someone who may or may not be dead. I took an 8mm camera with me while on some recreation while there and found that landscape intriguing—dark and foreboding. It was a good idea at the time."

I noted that the script did not waste a lot of time getting into things and our characters on to Caprona. "No, we did get right into it," Connor agreed. "By this time people had likely seen the first film, if they're fans of Burroughs or *Land*, they're going to know the situation. We didn't have to have a whole background of the characters, Patrick Wayne. It's an adventure and we can get through things like that with just a few lines. Get on with it."

McClure was no issue in returning. He had a good time with *Land* and *At the Earth's Core* continued his positive experiences with Connor as well as *Warlords of Atlantis*, so *People* was just a natural progression.

I did read the Burroughs book; The *People That Time Forgot* and looking back found major changes. McClure is reduced to an extended cameo in Connor's film, with him dying at the end to help the team that sacrificed everything to rescue him, leave him behind.

Bowen Tyler survived in the book, why didn't he in the film? Whose idea was that and to me, even as a boy felt the whole movie was kind of pointless when McClure died.

In a way it was like the killing off of Carrie Henn's Newt character from 1986's *Aliens* in its sequel, *Alien 3*, which rendered the entire plot of the previous film moot.

"I think that's why I wasn't so happy with the first draft of the script," Connor said. "That's why I wanted a go at it. I can't recall the original storyline but I know the McClure character was in it more. He was happy to return but John and Max said he would be relegated to the time he had."

Susan Penhaligon's character did not return and was killed off screen. "She didn't make it," McClure tells Patrick Wayne when found. We don't know what that means, but something happened. However, her character not only appears in the sequel book, she too makes it all the way to the end.

Was Penhaligon too busy? Was she even asked? She had made her way into television by the time *People* came about; maybe it had something to do with scheduling. "I don't really know why Susan didn't return," Connor confessed. "She just wasn't written in to be honest. The version that eventually came to me she had been written out. I have no idea if she wanted to do it or not."

I did say I read interviews where she said she wasn't asked but Connor couldn't confirm or deny. "Sometimes it's just the way life works out. Everything was very friendly and nothing negative toward her. A shame, I enjoyed working with her."

I asked about the budget because from my point of view, *The Land That Time Forgot* was a financial success. Connor cleared up the fact that while the original did do well, it didn't do THAT well to change his life or career. It did hit in the upper numbers of the UK boxoffice, but for Connor, he sees the original film as a modest hit.

He was also seeing it through eyes of an adult and I was seeing it through the eyes of a boy who judged success on how much I liked something and how many kids talked about in school.

The two do not correlate.

"We had some more money but it wasn't a lot. You can see from the cast, it wasn't an expensive cast. It was studio location even though we had some big builds on the sets. It was not a five million film. It was likely around 2-3 million at the time. Sarah Douglas hadn't done *Superman II* as of yet, but we had a wonderful cast with some great English names."

Connor did allude to the "fuzzy math" studios are known for with accounting film profits. While he had a "piece of the action" for the profits of *Land*, to this day he has never seen a royalty check.

"Things happen over time, libraries get sold, rights transfer and what are you going to do? You'll spend a fortune to figure it all out and often it's not worth it."

Would things be different this time around with the dinosaurs? Since *Land* we had the *King Kong* remake. Did that film bring Suitmation men in costumes back into vogue? Were the puppets considered to be replaced by men in suits?

1977 was the same year we got *The Last Dinosaur* for *ABC* television and it was a smash Friday Night Movie hit. That monster was suitmation, done by Godzilla effects artist Eiji Tsuburaya and his company.

Was it ever considered to use similar Japanese style suitmation this time around with the slight increase in budget?

"It was Maurice who thought to do *People* in costumes. This time we use small people for the costumes to move on all fours. We didn't do it for two-legged beasties, but rather for the four-legged ones as it allowed the actors inside to go a little longer as well."

The creature that came to mind was the hippo-looking type of dinosaur that comes after Patrick Wayne and his group when tied to the ground to be sacrificed. It bore a very strong resemblance to the creature Doug McClure killed in *At the Earth's Core* and turns out…it was.

At the Earth's Core saw almost all the monsters as suitmation which is why Carter had no issues in bringing it back for *People*.

"We did a lot more of people in costumes but it is exhausting and a bit slower because you can only do so much with the process. They had to be zipped up, form fitting and they couldn't breathe so well. We did a lot more in *Core* than we did in *People*."

Derek Meddings' son, Mark came on board to join the effects team. along with Dave Harris, John Richardson, Ian Wingrove. A solid group of people and so accomplished."

The mountain ranges for the opening flight into Caprona were also in the Canary Islands. Plates were shot from helicopter flying over them get the aerial points of view and backgrounds for the plane model and actor backdrops.

Connor paused here to talk about going for model shots without rehearsal. It was better to give it try and film and if it didn't work, you did it again. He was all for taking the risks and getting the shot. "You could get a great shot and miss it because you weren't rolling and taking it as a rehearsal. Just shoot it all," Connor told me.

The model work was all on stage back at Pinewood. The plane was a large model, on a sizeable set, operated with strings from above. "One time it came in, not as planned and ended up going up and over its nose."

I commented on the detail of the models this time around. The opening shots of the plane flying into Caprona entail a dogfight with a flying reptile. The dinosaur that scooped up Ahm in the first film, was pretty stiff and inflexible with a number of shots and cuts just to make it grab the caveman.

In *People* this winged beast cranes its neck, its eyes blink, the jaws open and close in the same shot without fancy cutting. Wrinkles are on the neck, looking like real skin—entirely different from its predecessor in *Land*.

"It was a beautiful model," Connor agreed. "It was big. All the little details and it had that working jaw. It had feathers and a lot more fine detail. The techniques improved in the years since land, especially in the armatures for the neck, etc. The model people made good use of it."

Connor had his original team intact, a perfect location and even Doug McClure returning.

Even with the new advances in dinosaurs, Connor was ready to move this sequel in a bit of a new direction.

Courtesy Tane McClure Arendts

Doug McClure with wife, Diane Furneberg whom McClure met onset while filming *The People That Time Forgot*.

MGM Studios

Courtesy Tane McClure Arendts

Kevin Connor (Center) with that giant functioning prop plane.

MGM Studios

MGM Studios

The flying reptile dogfight was a mix of projection, full-sized effects and model work, all brilliantly combined into a terrific scene at the start of the film and the team's excursion into Caprona.

This reptile was far more detailed than the one in Land.

MGM Studios

THE PEOPLE

Courtesy Kevin Connor

I asked about Patrick Wayne, legendary actor John Wayne's son; asking if he was cast to be a sort of "Doug McClure Light" kind of character. Tall, with rugged leading man good looks, Wayne seemed like the right actor who would have raised hell with McClure's Bowen.

Wayne, like his father and McClure, made his name in Westerns, appearing alongside his father at the age of 11 in *Rio Grande*. Throughout the 50s and 60s he went on to appear in *The Searchers*, *The Alamo* and *McLintock!*

He was no stranger to television, showing up on series work as well as game shows. He became a familiar face, that one where even if you didn't know his name, the moment you saw him, you were like, "Oh ! That guy!"

"We had such a great cast. We had such fun with the cast. The professor, played by Thorley Walters, was a particularly fun character and Walters was just a lovely, lovely man."

Walters' performance as intrepid, if sometimes daft, Professor Norfolk, echoed Peter Cushing's doctor in *At the Earth's Core*. Bumbling? Maybe, but brave? Absolutely. A gentleman? As only a British gentleman could be.

There was a darkness to the original cast in *Land* with the Germans and the whole war theme. This time we have a band of explorers of different personalities, with a few more quirks and character shadings than in the first film where it was basically McClure and McEnery shouldering most of the load.

There's more repartee tin *People* with Wayne and Douglas... the Jim and Pam...will they, won't they kiss and a smackering of *Romancing the Stone* seven years before that film came along.

Shane Rimmer's Hogan is the offbeat, rough and tumble pilot, Hogan who has some of the funnier lines in the film and has a real problem with those flying reptiles. He's relegated to stay behind with the plane to get it back in shape for departure. A shame, as I think his character could have given a lot of fun to the antics going on at the island's interior.

He does end up with the hot barbarian chick, Ajor (Dana Gillespie) in the end, so it's a wash.

The film would become notable for Sarah Douglas as she rocketed to fame a year later in her brief appearance in the first *Superman* film, but that movie was shot back to back with its sequel where she took the screen as arch villain and lover of General Zod--Ursa.

Take these colorful characters and shade them with an art design and costume design inspired by famous artists, Frank Frazetta, and you have a lot more going onscreen in this sequel. The look of it is entirely different than the first film yet it stays consistent in its feel and not separating from *Land*.

Dana Gillespie sported a hot cave woman Frazetta inspired barbarian outfit that Connor laughed and said the crew didn't mind and wished she ran and jumped around a little more because of how it revealed her shapely form. Frazetta wasn't known for his female subjects dressing modestly.

Coincidentally, I told Connor that I grew up in Stroudsburg and Frank Frazetta and his children lived in the neighboring town of East Stroudsburg and I knew them all.

Small world.

"John Dark and I were very accessible to the cast and crew while shooting. When at Pinewood we would have offices and always invite people to come by after shooting, let us know if they had any problems, that kind of thing. Every morning we would walk the departments and spend an hour, hour and a half to all departments to see how they were doing, invite them to come by at six o'clock to drop by our offices and let us know how they were."

People did. They DID come because they felt they belonged and treated well. "It was always a nice atmosphere and I encouraged that on every film I worked on."

I mentioned that again, Connor had famous franchise alum with *Star Wars*'s Dave Prowse who played Darth Vader. Connor's film also had poor Prowse under a mask and the actor lamented that.

"The fact that we could gather every morning and talk and have these after six meetings helped solve so many problems in advance. You saw everything in progress and could spot any issues way ahead of time before it was carried on the set as a big surprise. Nothing conflicted with the camera, the lighting—that kind of pre-production was always where you saved money, time and stress. It gave you more time to do more on the set and play around with things."

All of this showed onscreen with Connor's ability to extract so much production value despite the confines of budget.

A movie about dinosaurs depended on its people and the cast and crew were people that Connor and the executive team never forgot were the engines behind the entire process.

Courtesy Kevin Connor

Behind the scenes footage from Kevin Connor's personal "outtakes" reel showing the cast and crew between takes and working hard. Sarah Douglas gets a lesson from the tarantula wrangler.

MGM Studios

Courtesy Kevin Connor

PLACES AND THINGS

I marvel at the cavalier way films were made in the days before Internet saturation and the dissection of every molecule and piece of minutia for media scrutiny. Connor lobbed molten Styrofoam chunks at Doug McClure and Susan Panhaligon at the end of *The Land That Time Forgot*.

His crew swung large dinosaur models at actors from cranes and real oil was used for the oil pits in the film. With *People*, we get introduced to a large amphibious plane prop that, while it could not fly, it did sport a real propeller and those scenes where the actors are on that plane, that's a real blade going around.

Near the end of the film, Shane Rimmer is trying to jump start the craft, pushing the prop into motion and hoping it will catch the engine and start whirling. That's all real and that's the actual actor, not a stunt double handling a pretty dangerous piece of equipment.

All of this underscores the trust Connor had for his crew and the constraints they were under to get the film done on time and on budget. None of these events come even close to something like the 1983 tragedy of *The Twilight Zone* set accident, but it is amazing to a fellow a film director that there was such daring going on as the word "liability" kept popping up in my conversations with Connor.

There was no blue screen process with both films. The plates for the plane ride in were shot in Scotland. It was a mixture of both high sky shots and then when projected some smoke was waved in for the front projection proves to give some air turbulence in those shots.

While front projection sounds difficult, blue screening had its own problems which worked out over time until green screen took over.

The plane itself as a large prop was so textured and detailed. It LOOKED worn. "The plane was taken to the islands. It was made at Pinewood and we got hold of a transport plane that took all of us and the props and everything and we flew from England to Spain and directly to the Canary Islands."

The plane was broken down into pieces and reassembled on the island. "It was an electric engine, much like a fan for the propellers. Ian Wingrove helped construct it and design it. John Richardson and Dave Harris—they just did such wonderful work with models and miniatures. Great work."

The attention to detail was phenomenal.

When the plane first landed, the cast was in heavy winter jackets. The climate could not have been amenable to that. "The climate was lovely in the morning but as the day went on it go warmer because it was spring, you know."

The actors got out of those winter clothes pretty fast. "We never stopped for rain once. The weather was beautiful. It was the perfect time to go there."

I moved from the plane to the Stegosaurus scene which featured a variety of effects motifs to get that done.

The scene has the grounded plane stuck in a rock butte and the gang needs to free it. Sarah Douglas inadvertently finds a docile Stegosaurus feeding nearby and after pranking Patrick Wayne, he gets the idea to harness the giant beast to pull the plane free.

The creature was a combination of a full-sized prop tail, a scale model puppet and tied together between live action and rear projection.

"We shot the plates out there, but we did the model and puppet in the studio when we got back. Location work first. I mean we knew what a Stegosaurus looked like and what bits of the animal we would use on location."

The full tail was made of a rubbery material called "Sorbo" which has lots of air bubbles in it. It was easy to model and painted well. Johnny Richardson and the effects guys or electricians or crew not doing anything worked the tail.

MGM Studios

"We had the tail on a large pole and strong wire ran down the middle of the tail. Hands grabbed the pole and

MGM Studios

it was something to make the tail wiggle and twitch with some fine line as well. The boys constructed and painted it back in the studio."

The tail was rehearsed in England at Pinewood and when on location the effect came off without a hitch. "Pre-production!" Connor beamed. You can't underestimate the importance of pre-production.

The puppet-model of the Stegosaurus moved differently than the beasts in the first film. This one seemed more animated with some longer-holding wider shots to take the whole beast into frame. In the first film, there were lots of close-ups or medium shots from the bellies up, but we didn't see much of the legs moving or things like.

These large puppets had the main mechanism for the mouths and jaws operated like

Muppets as Connor said previously. The legs, however, were on sticks, and operated below the set, off camera out of frame to give the illusion of locomotion, that the animal was lifting its legs and walking.

The creature was not Suitmation, but instead an elaborate model-puppet that moved along a track slightly buried into the set. It was moved with the sticks and pulled by strings, hidden behind miniature rocks or darkened pipes buried into the set soil.

It was the first major terrestrial dinosaur in the film and Connor lavished considerable time on this set piece. Here we had this Stegosaurus moving over the land and the big budget *King Kong* remake gave us nothing like that. Maybe *Land* and *People* didn't have the budget but it had the creativity and inventiveness that a mega budget Hollywood film lacked.

"Given the budgets and so on, you really had to think out of the box," Connor conceded. "But I had such a great creative crew."

It showed.

The cast all got along. No behind the scenes drama and the closest to negative behavior was the kind of frustrations that just came from long days, heat, etc. "It was really like going on holiday," Connor laughed.

It was here he revealed he would often cut together a blooper reel of the shoots and then run the outtakes at the wrap parties for laughs. "I started this reel for *People* by saying "We are off to sunny Spain!" and we were…it was like going on vacation."

Kevin Connor sent me a blooper reel and some stills are published from it.

The director conceded that all sets have "That One" who could give a problem, but he shrugged it off. I replied that for me, the biggest problems usually came from the extras or day players who think they are the main attraction to the film.

I intimated to Connor that one film I did had the parents of two child extras ask if we could change our entire week's shooting schedule because they had a problem and wanted to change the shooting day so their kids could show up.

The answer was: "No."

The People That Time Forgot re-used sets from *At the Earth's Core*. "Maurice Carter was our production designer again for *People*. He more than likely used previously used sets because we didn't necessarily know we would use the same thing, but the goal was to save money. So we likely used some sets over, re-dressing them and making it all very efficient."

The scenes inside the mountain boundary where the team encounters a crawling rock monster, looked very much like the lava and crystal caves of *At the Earth's Core*. "Pinewood

MGM Studios

had detailed records of set docks which they just don't do today."

Connor again confirmed that the creature that came for Patrick Wayne and his team tied to the ground was a return from *At the Earth's Core* and indeed was suitmation with an actor inside.

"It's all about saving money but being as creative with that process as possible."

In many ways, *At the Earth's Core* could fit into this timeline and universe. It is its own film and a standalone story, but

232 • B. HARRISON SMITH

with just a few nips and tucks, it could have served as a prequel of sorts to *The Land That Time Forgot* and kicking off Bowen's adventures.

"It was magic. The magic of films," Connor confirmed. "I miss those days," he sighed.

As with all of my conversations, I so wished I could have been on Connor's sets to work and learn. This was the era I should've been making movies.

Connor's directing and filmmaking style took me back to my research on producers Arthur Rankin and Jules Bass who did numerous holiday TV specials, feature films and the subject of my previous book, *The Last Dinosaur*.

The associate producer on *The Last Dinosaur* told me that Rankin-Bass had their own way of making films. It was a relaxed kind of way where they got the projects done and done on time and they made money for the suits.

"They had a pedigree and were laid back," this producer told me.

Kevin Connor seemed to be cut from this fabric. Everything he told me, all of his accounts reflect a man who did not have to say he was the director or in charge.

A great phrase applies here: "If you have to say you're in charge, you're probably not." This applies to Kevin Connor who allowed his talented teams, crew and cast to do their thing, to make their magic and he supervised. He knew what he wanted to get onto the screen, but he trusted in his people to make that happen.

It all worked.

As I move into the final chapter of this remarkable era of film-making embodied by these two films, I encourage anyone who has seen either of these movies to give them a go and with all you've gleaned from this book, see more than what just made the screen.

There's history to this prehistory.

Courtesy Kevin Connor

A cast and crew group picture from *The People That Time Forgot* with Kevin Connor center.

Courtesy Kevin Connor

FAREWELL CAPRONA

The consistency between *Land* and *People* is integral to the success of these films. Utilizing the same team came from the terrible economic times of the early 70s which brought some of these huge names to the set because of the sheer desire to work.

Much of the matte work, which kept the look of the films unified, was done after the shooting of plates with the backgrounds composited in with running actors or creatures. The mattes were not painted on glass in the way Albert Whitlock would do them.

These effects are 50 years old and they still hold up. "They were tried and true," Connor agreed. "The technology got better and better and these effects guys were just dedicated to the film. They would do their magic for a fee, and on their time as long as they stayed on schedule."

I went back to Frank Frazetta and how the art design borrowed so much of the famous artist's work. I asked if they spent the money to license his work.

"Oh no," Connor chuckled. "I'm afraid not. We had artists do some knockoff work. We could never have afforded to license Frank Frazetta artwork."

If you look in the villain's lair at the end of the film where the sword fights play out you will see renditions of Frazetta's art hanging on the walls. One is so close to the famed Barbarian picture, I thought for sure it was licensed. Instead, it was just a "pretty close but not quite" copy.

The warlord costumes were all very Frazetta-inspired and gave pre-*Conan* vibes. "Oh yes," Connor said, "The Production designer knew of Frank of course. So he went for that look without copying. We were just cheating. Again, we could never afford to use the real thing."

The actor, Milton Reid, who played the green-skinned warlord, Sabbala reminded me Ed Wood favorite, Tor Johnson. The man's face, expressions and even the makeup took me right to *Bride of the Monster, Plan Nine From Outer Space* and other Ed Wood-Tor Johnson collaborations.

"No, I don't think it was a conscious thing on my part for that," Connor said. "The makeup department didn't decide to make him look like that. Milton Reid was also in *At the Earth's Core* as well. He wasn't consciously created not to look like Tor, but I agree he does look a bit like Johnson. I wish I could take credit for that but I wasn't as clever as that."

McClure's time onset was just under two weeks. "He was found at the end," Connor remembered. "It might've been a bit more with some leeway but he was part of the team and we did keep his character to a minimum because that's just the way it was written."

The total shoot was about six or seven weeks and McClure was there in a span over two weeks.

People had such a different look and feel. "Well it really didn't follow the book at all. If I had the energy I would like to get the rights again and do it properly," Connor confessed. "We did it from the script by Tilley and I am not sure how much of a hand in the rewrites Milton had in the script."

The goal was to keep the same overall style. "Why change it in a big way? We had the same art department team and set decorator so why change it overall?"

The new medieval type of elements fit well into the landscape as if we got a deeper look into Caprona's interior and more secrets held there instead of more cave men and such. We got something ambitious and cool that again seemed to set the stage for *Indiana Jones and the Temple of Doom.*

The volcano work was again high quality stock footage on 35 mm dexterously cut together with the stage and location footage. It is almost seamless to the point where I wondered if they had a model volcano but instead it was real footage shot in Hawaii.

The molten liquid in Sabbala's temple had a fiery moat of lava. I asked what it was made of. "Well, it was water with a wallpaper paste, this ingredient that got all gooey and filmy. You could put colored lights in it and it looked like it was flaming red hot. The substance had great reflective abilities but it was nothing more than a kind of clear wall paper paste. It worked so well and we used it a lot in *At the Earth's Core.*

It's here where I said again that this set and the fiery pit evoked *Temple of Doom.* "I never met Spielberg, unfortunately or ever had a conversation with him. Although I wouldn't be surprised if some of our effects boys worked with Spielberg because *Temple of Doom* was shot in England as well on set. George Gibbs is a name you'd want to cross reference.

Indeed Gibbs who worked on *People* did work on *Temple of Doom.* Did he bring the look of Sabbala's temple to the cult of Khali and Mola Ram? It's fun to think that and there had to be something to it.

There was such a big screen epic look to both *Land* and *People.* Again, Connor credited his crew and artists. "We had to fill the screen for a certain amount of money. We made the very best of what we were afforded. These guys were young—a new generation coming up and they brought their ideas and talents to the table."

The older crew and guys embraced it all and they worked together to makes such a great combination of older and younger generations. "Hopefully I had a bit of a hand in that as well," Connor was so humble.

I had to indulge myself with a silly question about Doug McClure's beard. Watching the film again, I was impressed with the realistic look of his facial hair. "Oh no," Connor corrected me, "that was his real beard. He grew that out for us!"

Connor was grateful McClure was so gracious because it saved an incredible amount of time in makeup, lighting, and continuity. "It was the same thing all the time, so we didn't have to worry about consistency." That was the editor in him coming out.

McClure returned to form in the fight scenes, especially the sword fights that took place in McClure's cell and the fire temple.

"I had no idea how to stage a sword fight. I had no idea. When I was an editor I would be given lots of shots and angles and takes with cutting it all together. You need a lot of rehearsal time. We used a sword master stuntman famous in England named Alf Joint. He was THE sword master. Whenever you had a sword fight he was the guy you went to and he was quite brilliant."

Joint worked in tandem with Peter Diamond in the stunts and fighting and it all came together. Joint's work also went into major films including *Goldfinger* and Connor was appreciative to have him for *People*.

I marveled over David Prowse's ability to lift Sarah Douglas right over his head in the sacrifice scene at the end. "She was a petite little thing," Connor chuckled. "I think I could've lifted her over my head myself."

Connor allowed Joint and Diamond to do their thing and did not interfere in the fight choreography. "What am I going to tell these men who are the experts in what they do? I had no experience in sword play or that kind of stunt coordination. My job was to make sure I got it all."

The run through Caprona, back to the plane was again dotted with fiery pieces of Styrofoam lobbed at the actors.

"Again, it was always a problem when those pieces bounced."

The actors had to run through a kind of mine field of pyro-technics at the conclusion of the film. The explosives were clearly marked for them, but camouflaged for the cameras. They knew which way to run and how much distance to keep between themselves and the charges.

Despite all of this, I thought the charges went off precariously near these actors. "No, they were all quite safe," Connor assured me. "Everything was clearly marked. Sometimes it was close but it was very nerve-wracking."

McClure was used to all of this from his war and Western work.

It looked like there were a lot more charges going off because three cameras were covering the same.

A stand out in the trailer that made me excited for this film was the giant snakes that burst from the walls. In the film they are a kind of guardian security system to prevent people from passing through this tunnel annex.

The snakes were all large puppets, operated by anyone on set who wanted to do it or were drafted. The eyes were lit with small lights to give an evil appearance. "We got guys and girls to stick their hands down these things. The actors ran through and they reached out to bite or grab them."

"It was so simple. You added some smoke, backlit the set with some glowing light and it came out great. It was a good time."

Toward the end of the movie, it seemed like a late, last act addition that "the land was alive." Patrick Wayne announced that they were being "chased by a volcano."

Where did that come from? Looking back at the first film, you could argue that Caprona didn't want the sub crew leaving either which is why the volcano stopped their exit.

I didn't remember this as part of the books and it was not talked about in any exposition in *Land*. Where did this concept of Caprona being somehow sentient come from and why introduce it into the third act as an almost kind of afterthought?

From a writing standpoint, why would the island allow anyone to enter in the first place? If someone did breach the defense, why didn't the island just kill them upon landing or arrival?

I got it that explosions and such make for an exciting ending, but couldn't it have just been another, periodic eruption? It all seemed like a plot point that didn't need to be there.

"I don't think it was from the book. It was in the script and I don't know if I put it in or not but I liked it. I liked the idea of the volcano and lava having kind of tentacles to reach out to keep you in, to block you. It was always interesting to see the land moving, pushing people away, in landslides, rocks slides. It's like Mother Nature telling the human race a few things and it's little stuff like that that I like to put into my films whether people pick up on it or not."

With flying fire blobs and explosive charges, I asked about the arrows used at the end in the standoff between the team and the Skull Castle warlords.

"They were real arrows," Connor conceded. "They were rubber but if you turned at the wrong moment they could likely poke your eye out."

I brought up the shot where McClure was pinned down between these rocks and hit with a volley of arrows. They hit like real wooden ones but the SOUND of them hitting the rocks sounded like the real deal. Was that real sound or added foley later?

Regardless, McClure gives a look like 'Damn! That came close!"

Connor laughed at this. "There might've been a mixture of rubber and wood. I think it depended on the shot for which was used. It depended on how close those arrows were to the actors. I am always scared about injuries on sets. We used to hand the bows and arrows to the electricians and riggers on the crew to shoot the actors. We might've had some stunt guys firing them but there was always a strong safety element."

McClure's death disappointed me as a boy. "I don't know why that decision was made. It had been made when I was handed the script and I went with it."

Bumping McClure off was a closure to his story. "Today he would've had ten sequels and three spin-offs," Connor mused. "I went along with it. I should read that script again."

McClure didn't put up any protest to being killed off. "Not that I recall," Connor remembered. "We just did *At the Earth's Core* and I think he was fine with that."

Was there ever a third film thought for this? Was there interest by the studio or distributor for a third one?

"No," Connor said. "We were going into the *John Carter* books and thought we were moving on to fresh material. The costs nipped that in the bud. The licensing fees were way too much. "When *John Carter* went away we thought around the table, why don't we do our own action adventure science fiction? That's how *Warlords of Atlantis* came up. We wrote that quite quickly and shot that right on the heels of *People*."

McClure would star in that one as well and will be covered in Volume II of this series.

"We moved straight into it. The economy was still very bad, so we moved into these films and were very lucky. That's again how I managed to get these great technicians because everyone wanted to work."

Connor was pleased to attend a recent showing of *Land* and *People* at Quentin Tarantino's theater in Los Angeles.

We ran the gamut…from the inception of *The Land That Time Forgot* all the way through *The People That Time Forgot*. Kevin Connor's work influenced my childhood and my dream to become a filmmaker and as I peeled back the layers to the making of these films, I saw why…he found good people and held on to them for life.

Caprona would not be the end of Connor's journey.

He would travel to earth's core then Atlantis and then circle back to his horror roots with *Motel Hell* and once again thrill me at the same drive in where I saw *People* and *Core*.

Kevin Connor made me dream bigger than the budget.

Courtesy Kevin Connor

Courtesy Kevin Connor

MGM Studios

Top L-R: Sarah Douglas, Patrick Wayne, Doug McClure, Dana Gillespie.

Middle: Dave Prowse, just before Vader's life support lifts Dana Gillespie over his head in the warlord arena.

MGM Studios

Bottom: Look closely to the artwork on the left and right and you will see the Frank Frazetta mock ups. The photo on the right resembles Frazetta's famed barbarian on horseback.

MGM Studios

MGM Studios

Tor Johnson

MGM Studios

Bowen Tyler (Doug McClure) and Ajor (Dana Gillespie) are 'The People That Time Forgot'... 1.15.

Mubi.com

Milton Reid

Milton Reid's Sabbala bears more than a passing resemblance to famous Ed Wood actor, Tor Johnson.

MGM Studios

AFTER THOUGHTS...

There is a major difference between "so bad it's good" and just plain "bad." We have lost sight of that in our entertainment, politics and even our education. Critical thinking has eroded while knee-jerk, emotional reactions and "put downs" are the standard for winning what used to be logical debate and educated conversation.

My first book looked at the history of horror through the theatrical and group experience and how the genre brought us together. Its title came from the tagline for what I consider the worst movie ever made, *Jaws the Revenge*. I won't go into detail here as you can see why I feel this way in my book, but *Jaws the Revenge* is not a movie. It was a cash grab, a tax write off, an excuse to spend money in a budget to extract some pay days and a three month vacation to The Bahamas.

Many try to argue that the third film in the shark series is hands down the worst, but I disagree. I believe director Joe Alves had no intention of making a bad film with his *Jaws 3-D*, but on the flipside I don't think anyone at Universal cared if they were making anything remotely close to good with *Jaws the Revenge*.

The conscious choice to make inferior entertainment, despite having the financial, creative and other resources to do otherwise is what I call *Cynema*. It is a term that fuses cynicism with cinema and sadly most of the "content" we see today falls under this category.

Martin Scorsese just this morning made another plea to save cinema from super hero claptrap and "theme park ride" motion pictures. He's not wrong. He's not an old man shaking his fist at clouds or yelling at kids to get off his lawn.

One of the greatest film directors is right.

I will classify *The Land That Time Forgot* and *The People That Time Forgot* as cinema. They are art and this entire book conclusively proves that. Both films were crafted by A-list artists who came together for the intent to make the best picture they could with the resources given.

They went beyond that and they were led by a director who loved film and understood it and knew that if these people are the best of the best, then they should be allowed to perform as such.

We have two films that transcend their budgets and even the expectations of their distributor, Sam Arkoff who prided himself in delivering "dreck." Once asked by famed film critic Rex Reed how Arkoff managed to squeeze out a terrific performance from Michael Moriarty in the giant flying lizard monster movie, Q, among a story laden with dreck, Arkoff replied, "Well, the dreck was my idea."

Ed Wood once sat in his apartment making alien spaceships from hubcaps and pie tins. Despite his limited budgets, I don't think it was Wood ever thought, "How can I screw the audience and fleece them."

Executives today can't say that.

While several of Connor's films have made it to the *Mystery Science Theater* lineup, they are even MORE enjoyable because they were so goddamned fun in the first place.

Several other films made by a company known for its Cynema dreck have films on there and there is no joy or much laughter watching those episodes because the original movies themselves were just cynical shit to begin with and zero fun.

Mac and Me plays in the same season as *The Land That Time Forgot* in the eleventh season of *MST3K* and I can tell you firsthand, the episode is only funny when the troupe acknowledges the abject cynical machinations behind the making of the blatant *ET* rip off and 90 minute commercial for *McDonalds*.

It's not funny. It's awful.

I was seven years old when I saw *The Land That Time Forgot* and I left that theater excited and thrilled. I went back to it after my disappointment with *King Kong* two years later.

I got that excitement again, now as a filmmaker after talking extensively with Kevin Connor for this book and wishing for those days to return.

Never forget this era of filmmaking. Never forget your dinosaur (or lose it).

Never forget filmmakers like Kevin Connor.

They are cultural treasures.

B Harrison Smith

Printed in Great Britain
by Amazon

36412951R00139